D1766627

HR FOR CREATIVE COMPANIES

KATE MARKS

RIBA ᵻᵻᵻ Publishing

HR for Creative Companies

© RIBA Enterprises Ltd, 2016

Published by RIBA Publishing, part of RIBA Enterprises Ltd, The Old Post Office, St Nicholas Street, Newcastle upon Tyne, NE1 1RH

ISBN 978 1 85946 593 6

Stock code 84265

The right of Kate Marks to be identified as the Author of this Work has been asserted in accordance with the Copyright, Designs and Patents Act 1988 sections 77 and 78.

All rights reserved. No part of this publication may be reproduced, stored in a retrieval system, or transmitted, in any form or by any means, electronic, mechanical, photocopying, recording or otherwise, without prior permission of the copyright owner.

British Library Cataloguing-in-Publication Data
A catalogue record for this book is available from the British Library.

Publisher: Steven Cross
Commissioning Editor: Sharla Plant
Production: Richard Blackburn
Designed & typeset by Studio Kalinka
Illustrations by Peter Harpley
Printed and bound by: CPI Group (UK) Ltd, Croydon, CR0 4YY

While every effort has been made to check the accuracy and quality of the information given in this publication, neither the Author nor the Publisher accept any responsibility for the subsequent use of this information, for any errors or omissions that it may contain, or for any misunderstandings arising from it.

www.ribaenterprises.com

CONTENTS

FOREWORD

Every practice is as successful as its people. We are in the business of designing for the success of our clients, so we should look after our own staff with respect and dignity in order to ensure our own business success.

I have been involved with the RIBA in several guises, including as Champion for Equality and Diversity, which is a central tenet of HR. As President of the RIBA, I believe we need to focus on inclusion in architecture. It is vital that we improve pride in the profession along with diversity and, of course, profit.

Architecture is facing a number of challenges; not least of these is how we treat our people. We need to concern ourselves with retention, to address the crisis of talent that we are currently experiencing, and to engender a greater spirit of collaboration through diversity.

We can only do this by adhering to not just good practice, but best practice measures to manage our people. Too often we have heard of a talent drain as people leave the profession for more opportunities in other sectors or other countries.

This publication is ideally positioned to help those of us who wish to introduce processes which will help to achieve these goals. Architecture is about people, by people and for people. We need to lead by example and provide workplaces where talent and creativity can thrive.

This book provides industry specific guidance to enable practices of all sizes to do just that. It offers practical and useful advice on each aspect of HR in a structured way that is simple to implement. The anecdotes and case studies add humour and a spark of recognition to those of us who work in the profession.

Read this book. Keep it for reference on the shelf in your office and direct anyone who manages a practice (and its people) towards it. It is an effective tool to help us achieve the profession to which we all aspire...

Jane Duncan
President RIBA

SERIES EDITORS' FOREWORD

Architects are in the business of creating enriching environments and stimulating spaces for their clients. It is surprising therefore that few design businesses fully understand the social, emotional and existential needs of their own people. *HR for Creative Companies* is an essential 'aide memoire', for the architectural library, for practitioners that aim to look after the real gold within their practice, their people.

It is in the interest of your business for your employee dealings to be as successful as they can reasonably be. Good human relationships create loyalty and the right motivations for staff to give of themselves, being the difference between a practice that is just surviving and one that is flourishing.

HR for Creative Companies identifies the cultural boxes that many architects know exist within the profession and levels off inconsistencies, through the role of an industry sensitive HR eye, with advice that qualifies more as a good practice guide. In doing this the author identifies the common HR health checks that need to be in place so that the practice and its leadership are protected.

The role of HR in architectural practice is ultimately twofold, to help manage and maintain the workforce, making sure that the 'human' aspects of your business comply, whilst from a commercial perspective keeping a keen eye on the 'resources' aspect of employees as being productive and profitable and knowing how to deal with them when they are not.

Through humour and an abundance of specific tips within the field of Architectural HR, this publication educates practitioners through anecdotal case studies from design practice and with up-to-date legislation aims to give practical advice. All of which will enhance your business and make it run smoother.

The publication has specifically been written in clear English with practical, applicable tips to help you attract, motivate and retain the greatest talent so you can focus on what you went into business to do, which is provide the best design solutions for your clients.

Del Hossain and Anne Markey

ABOUT THE AUTHOR

Kate Marks is the founder of EvolutionHR, a consultancy specialising in providing human resources (HR) support to small and medium-sized enterprises (SMEs) in the built environment sector. She is a Specialist Practice Consultant to the RIBA, and is a visiting professor lecturing in HR-related topics at IE Business School Madrid, University of Westminster and London Metropolitan University. Kate also teaches HR for the British Institute of Facilities Managers' vocational qualifications.

Kate has an MBA from London Metropolitan University and is a Chartered Fellow of the Chartered Institute of Personnel and Development (CIPD). She was formerly European HR Director of one of the largest architectural firms in the world, and has worked across the globe advising on people matters.

ABOUT THE SERIES EDITORS

Anne Markey is a director of Phelan Architects, a practice she founded in 2009 with her husband Brendan Phelan. She also heads up the Projects Office within the Sir John Cass Faculty of Art, Architecture and Design at London Metropolitan University, and has over twenty years experience as an architect. Anne is a member of the RIBA and sits on the RIBA CPD Sub-Committee. She is a board member of Catalyst Housing, one of the leading housing associations within London and the South East, where her role is that of Design Champion.

Del Hossain is the MD of the Adrem Group a leading International Architecture and Design Careers Agency based in London, Dubai and Shanghai. By background he is an Architect having practiced with some of London's leading design firms including Foster and Partners and ORMS. In 2012 he was Awarded 'London's Business Mentor of the Year' for developing companies with a social agenda and progressive ambitions. Del is also a qualified Organisational Development and Wellbeing Psychologist and works closely with leadership teams and Directors in the Creative Industries on their People Strategies and team motivation. He is also a speaker at numerous universities and a former Chairman of the Bartlett Alumni. Del is the Joint Editor of the RIBA's Business Books Series.

ACKNOWLEDGEMENTS

I gratefully acknowledge the hard work, patience and persistence of Sharla Plant and Sarah Busby (both formerly of RIBA Publishing), Anne Markey, Richard Blackburn and Jo Harwood in taking this book from an idea to reality.

I also thank those who have acted as 'guinea-pigs' in reading firsts drafts and offering feedback on tone, flow, consistency and grammar – most notably, Simon Jones and Niki Winsor. And, Peter Harpley's inspired interpretation of my hieroglyphics into contemporary illustrations is also recognised with thanks for his patience and skill.

This book would never have been possible without the clients with whom I've worked over the years.

They remain a never ending source of inspiration and learning. And, my colleague, Niki Winsor, deserves a medal for putting up with me as I gave birth to this book! I also acknowledge the input of Del Hossain whose perception, industry knowledge and friendship remain a boon.

Last but by no means least, I'd also like to thank the incoming President of the RIBA, Jane Duncan, for helping the HR cause by taking a stance on diversity and equality that aims to bring the humanistic aspects of the profession into the present day. Having spent a number of years orbiting the architecture world, I'm proud to be involved with this publication and hope that it serves to enhance the links between people and practice.

DEDICATION

To Laurie Dreyer, HR professional extraordinaire. For inspiring me to see beyond what I thought were the mundane operational aspects of HR and to champion its true value in any organisation. For helping me to keep the HR faith!

INTRODUCTION

The premise behind this book is that human resources (HR) and creative companies can work well together. Gone are the days when there was perhaps a lack of mutual understanding. Over the past few years, people have come to realise that HR can be a positive force within a creative company.

In the past, it was suggested that creativity would be hampered by the rules and regulations, restrictive procedures and narrow-minded approach of the HR practitioners. Clearly, historically, this may be the fault of the HR professionals themselves. But I propose that it is rare that a conflict is the fault of one party alone. The challenges of recent years have meant that HR can be seen in a more positive light as a true support and a valuable asset for companies in the increasingly competitive marketplace.

In this book I intend to show how HR and creative companies can work well together. HR can and should be a support to all companies and can enhance the very creativity that HR may perhaps have limited or hindered in the past. I also use the book to illustrate how the architecture profession has evolved and is still evolving in its attitude and approach to people management.

In Chapter 1, I give a brief overview of the architecture profession. The variety of forms in which architecture is practised mirror those of other creative companies. In turn, the form in which you choose to work will affect the way you interact with HR: what your needs might be and how those needs could be fulfilled. Not every company needs a full blown HR department. It's all about what support you need and where you can find it.

As I discuss in Chapter 2, it is only relatively recently that HR has been accepted as a profession as such; and HR itself comes in many forms. It's important that you give some thought to the best structure of HR for your particular company and, in this chapter, I have tried to provide some insight into what the options may be.

Each following chapter focuses on a different aspect of the 'employee lifecycle'. Even though an employee's time with a company is a continuum, it is easier to illustrate – from an HR perspective – if it is divided into sections. So, each chapter has a particular emphasis. These reflect the path that an employee might take, from first joining the company to their possible departure. Each chapter is intended to be of practical use rather than simply expounding theoretical models. Where possible, I've used case studies and notes to illustrate and enhance the key points.

You will notice that the chapters dealing with the start and end of the employee lifecycle with your company are the largest. As I'll discuss in more detail in Chapters 3 and 7, the interaction with the marketplace at these points is so important that it is essential to get it right. There are many considerations to be aware of and which will affect your own actions and behaviour. I've endeavoured to make these as clear as possible.

Chapters 4, 5 and 6 all cover different aspects of people management once your employee is safely ensconced in your studio or office. How to keep the ones who are an asset to your company, how to manage those who may not be – in essence, helping you towards the goal of having the right people in the right place at the right time.

This book is not about dumbing down HR, but making it more user friendly. As a creative professional you do not need to be an HR expert, but you will benefit from being aware of the possibilities available to help you run a business that gets the best out of your most important and expensive investment – your people.

Creative companies themselves are very often small and medium-sized enterprises (SMEs) founded by one or two talented individuals who wish to pursue their own path and establish their own brands. I agree with the CEO of a major industry body who said recently that SMEs are the engines of growth: they are the future of the UK economy.

The effects of the economic downturn since 2008 on creative companies have been massive across the board. This is true of interior design, architecture, graphic design, fashion, media, film, animation or any other of the myriad of creative ventures that the UK sprouts. Different industries may have suffered or have been affected in different ways, but all have been driven to consider their approach to work and to their competitors, and in doing so, their people.

The challenges of the past largely centred around how the necessary procedural aspects of HR can possibly, fruitfully and positively be married with the creative process. It is my belief that true creativity needs some element of grounding to flourish, certainly within a commercial context.

HR can provide that grounding and support. As a function, it manages your reputation in the marketplace, it manages risk in the respect of potential legal challenge and it enables you to attract the brightest and best talent to enhance your creativity and serve your clients better.

Yes, possibly, this is 'HR Utopia' that I'm describing. But it is no less possible for all that.

This book will focus on certain broad themes. It is not intended to be a list of rules and regulations or a series of procedures. It is written with an awareness of the creative mind, and tries to tread a delicate path between the need for certain structure, and the flexibility to exercise true creativity.

LOOK OUT FOR THESE ICONS

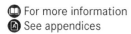

For more information
See appendices

THE PROFESSION

THE PROFESSION

These observations are the result of more than twenty-five years of working with, and learning to understand, admire and respect architects.

Architecture as a profession seems always to have been dogged by contradictions. It is a profession, but in comparison with others, is sometimes less well paid and often doesn't have the respect it deserves. In general, architects are highly intelligent and well educated; they love debate and sometimes love that debate as much or more than its purpose. In fact, architecture can be seen as a calling rather than a profession. At least, that may be one reason for a lack of commercial awareness. How many project budgets suffer from the hours of over- and re-design? And there are few other jobs where working through the night is seen as an acceptable and even necessary rite of passage.

The architecture profession has been through many changes in the past twenty years. These have included an increasing self-awareness and a genuine attempt to bring improved commerciality and business knowledge into the curriculum. This thrust has been long overdue, given that well over three quarters of architects will run their own business – it's a profession with many sole practitioners or smaller practices. Alongside the knowledge of finance, marketing and technology, HR plays its role in how a commercial practice should and can be run.

At the time of writing, things seemed to be developing well for architecture, but the effects of the recent recession have been far reaching. Records suggest that architecture suffered more job losses than any other profession during this time, and the number of architects claiming jobseeker's allowance (JSA) skyrocketed. The situation was similar for other property-, construction- and design-related professions.

Although the profession has matured, new challenges have arisen.
The need for flexibility, speed of reaction, versatility and commercial awareness has increased. From an HR perspective, it is heartening to note, for example, that HR is included in the Professional Criteria for Part 3 of the ARB. Knowledge of HR-related matters is specifically listed in three of the 50 criteria, namely: personnel management and employment-related legislation; staff development, motivation, supervision and planning; team working and leadership. It seems widely acknowledged that architecture at least, among the creative industries, is dependent upon managing people in such a way that they are able to explore their creativity.

📖 www.arb.org.uk

THE CREATIVE ENVIRONMENT

Although creative companies share many characteristics, there are also identifiable types. Ask yourself which one you belong to, because that will influence much of how you approach your staff and the whole issue of HR and people management.

Creative companies encompass a wide spectrum, ranging from architecture and interior design, product and graphic design, to fine art, publishing, fashion, music, TV and film. My own experience is largely with companies that could be described as being related to the built environment, so: architects, interior designers, product and graphic designers. Even so, there are many similarities across the spectrum.

Let's take a look at some common types of company in the architecture and design world and see if you can find one that best mirrors your own.

One man bands: not quite slaving over a drawing board or computer in a garret with a guttering candle, but the modern day equivalent. Driven by the desire to create and living from hand to mouth. This member of the species is common and often has to supplement more creative projects with house extensions or similar work to feed self and dependants.

Micro-studios: Started as a solo player and through luck, perseverance, talent or a combination of these, gained more lucrative or prestigious projects which have propelled the solo artiste to form a band of perhaps five or six people. Still probably working from the largest bedroom or a purpose-built extension of the owner's house. Looking to make the leap to their own premises. An exciting place to be, where hope is high and the possibilities endless.

Small to medium boutique design agencies: Often started by a few friends from university or a family-based partnership. They have a strong brand and want to keep it that way. The founders will be supported by a young and enthusiastic team of

2

juniors, largely straight from university. Very much driven by the mindset and ethos of the founders, but still desperately clinging on to the concept of creativity, client response and flexibility. Beginning to realise why the companies that they left to set up on their own had so many policies and procedures in place. Have experienced their first 'rogue' employee and are conscious of the time, cost and repercussions involved.

These three will form approximately 85 per cent of design practices.

However, the size and influence of the remaining 15 per cent is significant. These can be classified in several ways.

The 'names': As it suggests, the name of the practice reflects the names of the owners or founders. Now rather cynical and jaded, they have developed a successful practice over 10 or 15 years and have put in place the next level of management so that they can still focus on design while someone else does the day-to-day running of the company. They have developed a niche portfolio in a couple of sectors which provides them with regular workload and income. They've grown to employ perhaps 25/30 staff and it looks as if they may need to grow further. This is a slightly frightening prospect and they suspect it may have implications of some sort in terms of employment and responsibility towards staff, but there is no urgency to look into it. The next level of management will do so for them. They may develop into …

Black cape architects: Founded by a famous individual, usually male, and rather orientated around his personality, ego and lifestyle. This is what most architecture students assume they will be or dream of being before the harsh reality of life in the architecture profession hits them. Highly successful in the commercial sense or in their profile, these individuals will die in harness through a combination of ego and failure to provide for the future. The attraction of working for one of these practices is to have the name on your CV. It is likely that you will learn a lot about the creative process simply by hanging on the coat tails of this famous individual, but it is equally likely that this is an unrealistic way of directing your career: your own chances of developing your own design profile are more limited, or you may not be as talented as the individual concerned.

Cooperative: Some SMEs may go down this route, for instance, where the company ethos began with 'we all studied together and got on well, so let's start a business'. This may sound like the practices described above, but it is different in that it has kind of settled into itself. There was no ego strong enough to wish to become a black cape architect. Those who founded the company, hired staff and acted as mentors to hone their design talent and management skills. A very egalitarian company where the founders do not take exorbitant salaries or take all the kudos for the work produced by the practice. They still enjoy what they do and pass on this love of design throughout the company. Graduates and less experienced staff members love it and learn a lot. These companies save the tortured souls that emerge from university wanting to change the world and help them to find a way to make a difference or make their mark

without needing to have their name in lights above the highest building in the world's national capitals.

Business disguised as 'design': Big, big, big, except when the economy crashes and they cut their cloth (and staff) accordingly. Often international, they see no limit to their horizons. Probably the most commercially astute, they have robust systems and procedures in place for almost every aspect of their work. Typically very competitive in their salaries and with good benefits and compensation packages. They may compromise on design and tend to be client focused rather than innovative. You need to be able to play the political game to get on, as well as developing the hide of a rhino. A great training ground, you're unlikely to fulfil your creative dreams here, but can make use of the generous opportunities for training and development to make some steps to your own self-actualisation.

Family: Tend to be long established with a broader demographic than most creative companies. They are able to engender a great deal of loyalty and long service. Their reputation as a caring company is not ill founded. However, the route to the top is likely to be through length of service. They are founded on a somewhat paternalistic hierarchy, almost like an apprenticeship scheme; you may hear: 'we had to do it, so they can too' regarding working through the night, hours redesigning lobbies and toilets, filing drawings, and so on. These companies provide perhaps a more secure working environment than most. Their designs and creativity are unlikely to set the world on fire, but are generally of a good workmanlike standard. Again, this

is a fine training ground for a structured approach to work. The law is unlikely to be broken ever because the level of risk is minimal.

These examples illustrate the wide variety of creative environments that exist. They also illustrate the vastly different approaches to people management that can occur.

No one type of working environment will fulfil the needs of all creative individuals. Ultimately, people generally gravitate towards the environment that suits them best and best enables them to express their creativity.

PEOPLE MANAGEMENT IN CREATIVE COMPANIES

Let's conclude this chapter by a few words about what this all means for people management in the architecture profession and other creative organisations.

Creative people need the space to be creative. However, if they have chosen to be engaged to work for you, you will inevitably have some kind of responsibility for them and this is where the restrictions resulting from that responsibility come into play.

You are faced with the challenge of legal compliance and good practice while trying to establish a working environment in which your most creative people can produce their most creative work.

I've been told by several creative people that one of their greatest challenges is managing themselves. They have all the great ideas but these can overwhelm them and – if left undirected – can simply result in chaos. The workplace provides an environment where ideas are channelled towards specific client projects. A structure is provided in which the creative person is guided towards completing a genuinely creative result.

Managing creativity without stifling it is certainly not easy. It is elusive and intangible. So, how do you create an environment in which creativity can flourish? It's not necessarily about providing brainstorming dens, or walls to draw on, or lights or images to stimulate. Here are some guidelines:

> **Avoid unnecessary bureaucracy**: Policies and procedures do not need to be onerous, they just need to work; there don't need to be hundreds of forms to complete. Working life does not need to be driven by documentation.

> **Consider the appropriate timing of control during a project**: The initial phases of discovery, innovation and design development will be hindered and restricted by too much control, but eventually the process does need to be managed from a commercial point of view. Think hard about how these two aspects can be balanced.

> **Facilitate input from diverse perspectives**: Be sure that your workforce is sourced from a diverse pool and use that diversity to enhance the creativity of your company. The creativity of your company will reflect the different sources of ideas and viewpoints of your people.

> **Act as a filter**: Your role as a manager or director of a creative organisation is not only to foster the creative environment, but also to sort the good idea from the bad, or recognise the commercially viable versus the wildly impractical.

> **Allow a safe place to fail**: Genuine creativity may need several attempts before it succeeds. You may have to live with several failures as part of the creative process before you reap the rewards of success. You can only benefit from your client's satisfaction with a truly creative response to their needs.

CURRENT FOCUSES FOR HR AND PEOPLE MANAGEMENT

There are numerous challenges in the current marketplace. Here are some examples that we will focus on in the following chapters:

Finding the right staff with the right skills: This has always been a necessity, but can involve varying sizes of pools of expertise because people may leave the industry in economic downturns due to lack of opportunity or other personal reasons. Although there may be a rush to recruit in some areas, there is also a keen search for specific skills. A lesson learned from the economic downturn is that companies are less likely to hire simply for talent alone with the hope that they can find somewhere to fit in the individual.

Keeping the right people: There is also a heightened desire to retain and develop the 'good' staff. Increased competitiveness as the market stabilises means that rival employers need to seek ever more innovative ways in which to hang on to the talents of those who exemplify the skills and behaviour they wish to support and perpetuate in their company.

Addressing below-standard behaviour: The other side of the coin to keeping the right people is managing those who may not be such an asset to your company. Although no one relishes difficult conversations, recessions do seem to teach companies that a problem ignored is a problem increased. There is a reluctant acceptance that the processes and procedures needed to address performance and possibly dismissal are there for a purpose and, although not to be welcomed, can be used to the advantage of the company. This helps you gain the workforce you need and want in order to produce the work that you wish to do for your clients. The beauty is that every company is different and someone who doesn't work well in one particular working environment may flourish elsewhere and vice versa.

Management skills/leadership: As all of the above points indicate, it's now even more the case that simply being a good architect is not enough to run a practice successfully. Some people believe that leaders are born not made; nevertheless, some basic training in management skills will help to prevent the major forms of bad practice, and will – ideally – engender an environment where your staff can flourish profitably to the benefit of your clients.

Succession planning: The profession has been notoriously vague about succession planning, albeit we have more recently seen some fine examples of how this has changed for the better. Nevertheless, architecture as a form of vocation does not lend itself easily to structured retirement, and that poses a challenge for the next generations and the future of your practice.

Without doubt, architecture and the creative industries are people orientated. Without the skills and knowledge of your people, you have no product and no business. Explore the chapters of this book to help you make the most of the talent that you have at your disposal.

WHAT IS HR?

It's not an exaggeration to say that mentioning you work in 'human resources' at some kind of social event causes a reaction similar to saying you work as a tax inspector or a traffic warden. We often seem to be seen as a necessary evil. Many are the tales of incompetence, insensitivity, slowness and lack of commercial understanding. Most people have their own negative experience with HR, ranging from a slow recruitment process to an impersonal and insensitive redundancy process. George Clooney's 2009 film, *Up In The Air* – in which the protagonist makes a living as the go-between who tells workers they have been 'let go' when their employers are unwilling to do it themselves – did us no favours.

There are a number of reasons why HR has a negative reputation and this is not the place for an in-depth examination of HR as a profession. Suffice to say that those whose role involves or whose job title includes HR can be from many backgrounds, with wide-ranging experience and with many or few qualifications in the field. HR as a professional career is relatively new. It has been through significant changes in the past few years and is now really coming into its own in proving the value that it can add to a company. It is beginning to be taken as seriously as finance, marketing and IT in boardrooms.

As a profession, HR has its house in order. It has a professional body, the Chartered Institute of Personnel and Development (CIPD). Basic membership is relatively easy, but the more senior levels of membership are only granted after proof of skills, qualifications and experience. This will all help to increase credibility over time. There is recognition that HR, when it is done well, is of immeasurable value to any company. We need more positive public relations because, love it or hate it, HR is here to stay.

However, it is likely that we will never be able to completely dispel the negative reputation. Who is it that will be involved with disciplinary matters, or performance management, or redundancies? Who is less likely to be involved with giving pay rises, or promotions, or handing out rewards? It is perhaps unsurprising that managers often like being involved with the positive aspects of dealing with people, but may delegate the aspects that are perceived to be negative.

Also, it will be an HR representative who is telling you when you can and can't do something in order to maintain legal compliance; hence, 'HR just keep telling me what I can't do'.

HR specialists are rarely involved in helping to create business strategy and so often are simply implementing someone else's plans whether they agree with them or not. They may feel a certain amount of resentment if they have no input into the decision-making process. This may come across as diffidence or defensiveness.

What we need to develop is a positive working relationship with HR. HR will watch your back in terms of legal compliance and warning you of likely legal challenges. HR will free you up to focus on your company's core business and why you started it in the first place.

HR will still come in many forms – see below and take your pick – but try to ensure that their role is varied and they are engaged with you and the company.

Every company is different and will have different focuses for HR. The first step tends to be legal compliance in the form of documentation. This is often simply making sure that there is a reasonably up-to-date contract of employment template and some basic policies in place. Some more daring companies might even go straight for having a more comprehensive employee handbook with a wider array of policies.

The next step is often designing an appraisal system that is appropriate for the company: then some management training in interviewing skills and how to conduct a disciplinary or grievance meeting.

It's very much a step-by-step process.

However, there remain many myths about what HR actually is or does.

I should allay any fears that this book is trying to teach you everything there is to know about HR; it is not. Instead, it will focus on what you need to know as owners, directors or managers of small and medium-sized creative companies. It will also guide you as to how to make the best use of HR within your organisation.

THE EMPLOYEE LIFECYCLE

Let's begin by clarifying what HR is and what it covers. Many people still associate it with hiring and firing. This illustration should help to connect the two.

THE EMPLOYEE LIFECYCLE

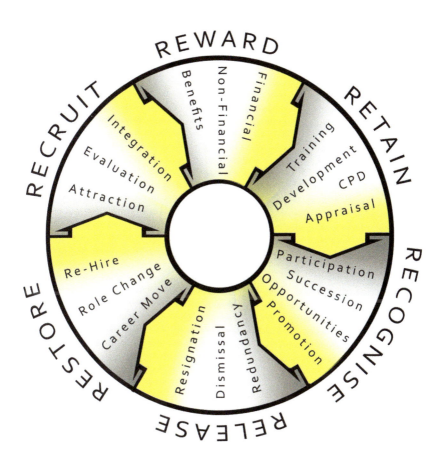

The employee lifecycle rather speaks for itself. It is a continuum from when the employee first approaches your company to apply for a job until they leave – and then perhaps return in the future to a new or similar role.

Recruitment (hiring) and release (firing) are certainly key aspects to what HR actually does. They are the main points at which the company interacts with the marketplace. How you choose to conduct these aspects of people management will tell the world much about your culture and ways of doing business. We will talk about the importance of your corporate brand in the next chapter, in relation to recruitment.

However, in terms of good practice and creating an environment where you have happy and productive staff, the points between recruitment and release are equally important. If your HR practices are not joined up and if they are inconsistent, they will be less effective and most likely more time consuming and therefore costly to you; not to mention opening up the possibility of problematic and even discriminatory practices. An example to which we'll refer again later, is the job description. Consistency in the use of job descriptions throughout the employee lifecycle makes your expectations clear right from the start and should make your life easier because of that.

So, there are HR-related responsibilities relating to your staff members even before they start working for you and also when they have left your employment, and all points in between.

Recruit:
> Attracting the best candidates that are right for your company

> Managing the recruitment process and ensuring effective recruitment methods

> Making offers of employment

> Ensuring orientation and a smooth transition into your workplace

> Managing the probationary period and being sure that it is used properly.

Reward:
> Ensuring a fair and competitive remuneration structure

> Resourcing a benefits package that reflects the company's budget and ethos

> Planning a clear articulation of what is rewarded in line with company culture and ethos.

Retain:
> Putting into place a well-considered retention plan

> Ensuring employee motivation and engagement

> Managing professional learning and development, using appraisals and other tools.

Recognise:
> Helping to articulate the basis for promotion

> Driving management training and leadership development

> Assisting in succession plans.

Release:
> Assisting in performance management plans
> Leading the disciplinary (and grievance) procedures
> Managing dismissals and redundancy programmes
> Supervising exit interviews and the resignation process
> Dealing with matters relating to former staff such as references and benefits.

THE HR SKILLS PORTFOLIO

There are many tasks and roles that come under the umbrella of HR. In larger organisations, the HR department can be huge and encompass a vast array of specialist HR functions: recruitment; training and development; compensation and benefits; employee relations; health and safety; reward and recognition; leadership/management development; and so on. In a smaller organisation, you may have only one person who is responsible for HR and who may also be carrying out other roles. In some of the smallest organisations, it is likely to be the managing director/senior partner/ owner in conjunction with their PA/ secretary/office administrator who does everything.

It is probable that a high proportion of SMEs will engage with an HR generalist rather than a series of specialists. An HR generalist, as the name suggests, has chosen not to specialise and so provides a broad range of services encompassing most of the functions relevant to the employee lifecycle.

The various roles that an HR generalist may need to adopt during their career can include:

> Sales – recruitment is as much about selling as buying; HR will be the first port of call and may be the first interaction that potential new recruits have with your company
> Counsellor – HR often provides the first port of call for issues that employees are experiencing, both personal and professional
> Hatchet wielder – leading dismissal procedures and redundancies
> Police officer – ensuring that the company operates towards its employees within the legal framework
> Negotiator – whether it be negotiating a good deal with benefits providers, training companies or managing an angry director who just wants to dismiss a poorly performing staff member: ensuring risk is managed by following a proper process
> Teacher – designing and delivering training or providing mentoring and guidance to managers in HR practices.

13

THE FOUR ROLES OF HR

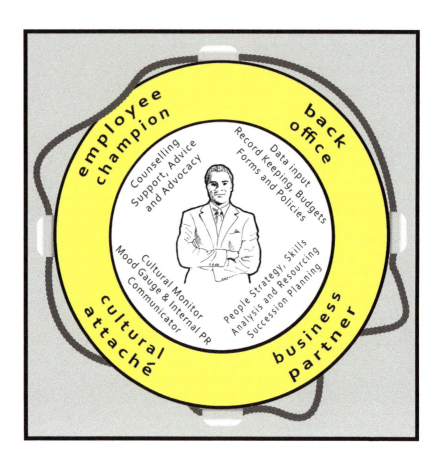

Back office: This is the administrative aspect of HR – inputting data, monitoring holiday and sickness absence, providing forms, explaining policies, managing budgets. It requires accuracy and a love of detail and process.

Business partner: This is how the people strategy fits in with the business strategy; making sure that there are the available skills in the company to fulfil business needs; resourcing, development and succession planning.

Cultural attaché: This person walks among the staff members, assessing the culture and how it is evolving, managing the myths and legends of the company; the conduit between management and staff.

Employee champion: This person provides counselling and support, guidance, mentoring, advice and information; ensuring fair and consistent business practices.

As you can imagine, each of these roles requires different strengths and characteristics. A successful HR professional has to be something of a chameleon. They need to be good at data input, figures and detail; to be sensitive, emotionally intelligent and able to put themselves in other people's shoes; to be pragmatic, business focused, commercially aware and a strategic thinker. HR professionals also need to know when to be flexible and when to stick to their guns. This variety provides both the challenge and the fascination for this profession.

BUILDING YOUR HR CAPACITY

I've often been asked for my advice on creating the ideal HR department. The answer will vary considerably from company to company.

The process should begin with taking a look at what resources you already have within the company. Someone among the staff may have legal knowledge, or training expertise. But if you are genuinely starting from scratch, there are a number of ways you can obtain the expertise that you need. I've already mentioned smaller companies where the MD's PA/office manager may fulfil the function. If you have only four or so staff, you really don't need a full-time HR expert. When you hire your first administrative staff member, make sure they are organised, intelligent, willing to learn, conscientious and thorough in their work. This will cover most of the clerical aspects of HR, such as personnel filing, employee information maintenance, sickness and holiday records, and so on. You can use external experts for support. This may be an HR consultant or occasionally an employment lawyer. You may also find that a consultant can provide some coaching in basic HR practice so that you can see the internal body of knowledge developing.

As you grow, you may feel the need for a part-time HR specialist and ultimately a full-time HR manager.

SMEs will be served well by an HR generalist. It is relatively rare for a creative company to have the resources or need for a department of specialists. Even working for a company with a few hundred people, a senior HR generalist, supported by a recruitment specialist, a training and development specialist, and a good administrator, worked well for me.

The responsibility for HR within smaller organisations will usually be shared between an HR representative and the managers. The representative will offer advice, guidance and support, but it is the managers who work with their staff on a day-to-day basis, who will know them best and who can be more sensitive to their individual motivations and needs. This is a partnership. HR will enable and facilitate; managers will manage people.

EMPLOYEE RECORDS

> Be sure to comply with the Data Protection Act – keep records confidential, up to date, and accurate.

> Keep any personnel files in a locked cabinet with limited access.

> There is no specific legal requirement as to what should be in a personnel file, but common sense suggests a CV, contract of employment, bank details and emergency contact as a minimum.

> Keep a simple spreadsheet of basic employee information for ease of use. You don't need an expensive or complicated database.

> Keep any documentation regarding performance, reward, training and development.

THE LEGAL BIT

When this book was first mooted, it was agreed that the legal aspects of HR were best dealt with in specialist texts – and they have been, most ably. However, there are certain key points which it is almost impossible to avoid when discussing HR. These particularly relate to the Equality Act.

📖 www.legislation.gov.uk

Much of this Act underpins all that HR professionals do, because it's all about treating people fairly and consistently. If you don't, you are likely to fall foul of the Equality Act and all that it contains.

There are two main aspects of the Act that you need to be aware of and which you should remember as you take a look at the rest of this book: protected characteristics; and types of discrimination.

Let's keep it as simple as possible.

There are nine protected characteristics and seven different types of discrimination. The key points are summarised in the tables below.

If you treat all your employees, potential employees and former employees fairly and consistently, the issue of discrimination and the spectre of the Equality Act need not arise. Keep these tables listing the protected characteristics and types of discrimination to hand as a useful reference in all your dealings with people.

It's also good to keep a check on your own attitudes and behaviour from time to time to be sure you are not inadvertently crossing the line. We are all subjects of our own prejudices and filters, but it is important to be aware of them and not apply them within the workplace.

	PROTECTED CHARACTERISTICS	POINTS TO REMEMBER
		A protected characteristic as defined under the Equality Act is a characteristic by which any discrimination would be unlawful
A	Age	This covers young as well as old, so be careful of long service awards. Remove references to retirement age from all contracts of employment and manage people based upon their performance not their age.
B	Disability	This refers to mental as well as physical disability; it may also encompass such wide-ranging conditions as multiple sclerosis, cancer, depression and dyslexia. Seek advice on this, because it is all to do with how the condition may affect the person's ability to work. You will hear the phrase 'reasonable adjustments' that may have to be made to accommodate a disability.
C	Gender reassignment	Do not confuse this with transvestism. A simple example: the comedian Eddie Izzard (transvestite) would not be protected, Kellie Maloney (the boxing promoter, born as 'Frank' Maloney) would be protected.
D	Marriage or civil partnership	Single people are not protected.
E	Pregnancy or maternity	Don't fail to include those on maternity/paternity leave in important communications about the future of the company or even in such significant matters as a redundancy programme that is going to affect all staff. To do so would be discriminatory.
F	Race or ethnic origin	Includes colour and nationality. Do not assume that Scottish people or English people are not protected. People from other EU countries are also protected.
G	Religion or belief	This must be a strongly held authentic belief. It includes philosophical beliefs such as environmentalism and also lack of belief, i.e. atheism.
H	Sex	As it suggests, a man or a woman.
I	Sexual orientation	Whether someone is homosexual, heterosexual or bisexual.

TYPES OF DISCRIMINATION	POINTS TO REMEMBER
A Direct discrimination	Simply, this is when someone is treated in a worse manner than others because of a particular characteristic (e.g. you didn't hire someone specifically because you thought they were too old).
B Indirect discrimination	For example, an employer could introduce a shift pattern which requires all employees to work until 10pm three times a week. However, women are going to be disproportionately affected by this because women are more likely than men to have caring responsibilities. How you treat part-time workers may also need consideration in this context.
C Associative discrimination	An example of associative discrimination might be not giving someone a promotion because you believe that the caring responsibilities they have for a family member will distract them from their new responsibilities.
D Discrimination arising from a disability	This is not simply about a disability itself, but about its effects. For example, someone might be treated less favourably because they have poor handwriting and make a lot of spelling mistakes. This could be discrimination arising from a disability if the reason for this was dyslexia and the dyslexia in this specific instance met the definition of a disability: 'A physical or mental impairment which has a substantial and long-term adverse effect on the person's ability to carry out normal routine activities.' You cannot ask health questions prior to employing someone unless it's for specific reasons, such as making suitable arrangements for interview.
E Perceptive discrimination	This is discrimination against a person because it is thought they possess that characteristic, even if they don't (e.g. someone who is thought to be gay but is not).
F Harassment and bullying	Harassment has a very specific definition: 'unwanted conduct related to a relevant protected characteristic, which has the purpose or effect of violating an individual's dignity or creating an intimidating, hostile, degrading, humiliating or offensive environment for that individual'. It is about how the person feels, not necessarily whether harassment was intended. Under the Act, employees can complain of harassment even if they don't possess the protected characteristic or the harassment is not directed at them.
G Victimisation	This has a very specific meaning. It is when an employee is treated less favourably because they have made or supported a complaint related to the Equality Act, or they are suspected of doing so.

CURRENT EMPLOYMENT MARKET

At the time of writing, the employment market in general is at the most interesting it has been for a long time. We appear to be emerging from what was, conceivably, the most challenging period in the life of many creative companies, especially those related to the built environment. So many companies have experienced redundancies, reduced hours and reduced salaries, cuts in training budgets, and the lack of productivity that fear for the future and insecurity can bring. Hence, the recovery has not been as bullish as it might have been in the past. It's almost like an animal emerging from hibernation blinking into the sunshine. There seems to be a hesitancy to make impulsive decisions, and a tendency towards rather more close deliberation and research before making a move.

There are perennial themes regarding HR and employment: these include the search for talent, hiring and developing the right people for your company, succession planning, and leadership. In some ways these are melded together, in that there appears to be a desire to get the best out of the existing staff – so, an increase in performance management measures and plans with a view to improving the skills and productivity of a team or finding a way to terminate their employment.

This is not to say that recruitment is not taking place. Certainly, the recruitment market is rather more buoyant as we move into the second half of the decade than it has been for some time; but seems to be more orientated around seeking specialist skills or strategic hires. It is widely reported that, although there are people seeking work, and increasing mobility from the European Economic Area (EEA) and other countries outside the UK, companies are trying to hang on to their good staff and so there is a mismatch between talent available and talent sought. We read in the newspapers that UK employees are the least productive in Europe and this concern is reflected in the apparent drive to develop the most well-rounded, multi-skilled, efficient and effective employees possible.

Developing your HR practices to echo these new priorities will enable you to achieve your goals. Read on!

RECRUIT

It may seem obvious, but 'recruitment' is the whole process that you follow once you've decided that you need additional resources. This includes where you find candidates, how you find them, the methods you use to decide if they are right for you, how you present yourself to them and how you entice them to your company. It also involves how you introduce them to your company and how you integrate them so that they are happy, productive and want to stay.

Is it that easy? Of course not!

Recruitment is one of the most volatile and changeable activities that HR professionals are involved in. It sometimes seems as if almost every architect's practice has either too few or too many staff. As we know, despite the challenges of the recent economic downturn, there is always a certain amount of mobility between companies as individuals find the place where they feel most creative and which suits them best as a working environment. So, let's talk about how we go about recruiting successfully.

Firstly, you need to look at this process as a two-sided activity. You have a need; your candidate must want to fulfil that need. It's not only about what you want, but what they want.

In other words, even though you have a project role that needs to be filled, you also have to consider what's in it for the potential applicants.

Secondly, it's often the case that recruitment is something of an emergency decision. I'm sure you can imagine the meeting where someone says: 'We've got loads of bids out there and if we get all the work in, we don't have enough staff to do it.' In such a case, you could end up panic buying. To avoid this, be sure to follow a sequenced process.

This chapter breaks down the recruitment process into a series of manageable steps, and also provides some guidelines on the process of selection and rejection, and what needs to be done to help your new recruit during the all-important induction period.

1. IDENTIFYING A NEED

As with most project- and people-related matters, a bit of forward thinking and preparation will save you much time and avoid many problems in the future – it doesn't matter whether you call it HR planning, resourcing or project planning.

Don't simply wait for a large project to arrive in your office. An important part of running an office is to ensure that you continually monitor whether you have the right people with the right skills and aptitudes to do the current and forthcoming work. Some of this may be guesswork, but if you use a mixture of information from past experience combined with common sense, you will be better prepared. Even in HR theory, the most common method of HR planning presented is that of 'managerial judgement' – in essence, this is simply making a theory out of practical experience. There's no magic to it.

Use your own past experience and as much knowledge as you have of future company plans and workload. This may be as simple as running through the influencing factors, as illustrated overleaf.

In particular:

> Match the need against your existing staff and their skills.

> Consider the career and development aspirations of your existing staff.

> Consider training your existing staff to fulfil the need.

Do not forget to also consider other factors, particularly the possibilities of:

> Internal movement – role change, promotion, other internal movement from existing to new role.

> Leavers – returning to university, end of work permit, relocation, resignation.

> Requests for flexible working – carers, parents, staff approaching retirement or needing to study.

> Returning to work – end of maternity leave, study leave, travel, sabbatical, leave of absence.

> External factors – holiday periods, financial cycle, cash flow, software upgrades, seasonal influences.

> Staff numbers – understaffing (requiring recruitment/selection) and overstaffing (requiring redundancy/termination/reduced hours/leaves of absence/reduced pay).

BEFORE RECRUITMENT
ESTABLISHING IF THERE IS A NEED

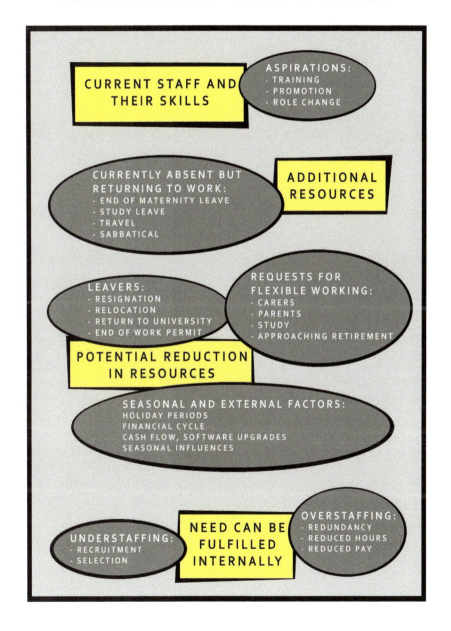

CURRENT STAFF AND THEIR SKILLS

ASPIRATIONS:
- TRAINING
- PROMOTION
- ROLE CHANGE

CURRENTLY ABSENT BUT RETURNING TO WORK:
- END OF MATERNITY LEAVE
- STUDY LEAVE
- TRAVEL
- SABBATICAL

ADDITIONAL RESOURCES

LEAVERS:
- RESIGNATION
- RELOCATION
- RETURN TO UNIVERSITY
- END OF WORK PERMIT

REQUESTS FOR FLEXIBLE WORKING:
- CARERS
- PARENTS
- STUDY
- APPROACHING RETIREMENT

POTENTIAL REDUCTION IN RESOURCES

SEASONAL AND EXTERNAL FACTORS:
HOLIDAY PERIODS
FINANCIAL CYCLE
CASH FLOW, SOFTWARE UPGRADES
SEASONAL INFLUENCES

UNDERSTAFFING:
- RECRUITMENT
- SELECTION

NEED CAN BE FULFILLED INTERNALLY

OVERSTAFFING:
- REDUNDANCY
- REDUCED HOURS
- REDUCED PAY

CHECKLIST FOR RECRUITMENT

> Be sure there is a need for the role – project, sector, skills.

> The role may be specific to a project, may supply longer term skills or may fill a more strategic management or leadership requirement.

> Never forget or overlook internal resources and be sure that the role cannot be fulfilled internally, possibly with guidance or mentoring, enabling your staff to take steps along their chosen career path.

All these considerations will help you to decide who you are really looking for. Once you've done that, prepare a job description.

2. WRITING A JOB DESCRIPTION

Job descriptions are sometimes thought of as restrictive, inflexible and a possible excuse for the old adage 'it's not in my job description'. However, they are one of the main building blocks of good HR and your ability to manage people consistently and effectively.

A job description used for recruitment need not be an exhaustive detailed list of tasks. Instead, it should be a guide to main responsibilities, reporting lines and expected outcomes of the role.

The job description helps you to obtain applications that are actually appropriate for what you want, it will be a prompt for you in your interviews, it will help to ensure that the expectations of the role are clear from the outset, it limits misunderstandings and enables you to manage performance well and reward success. It may not be the solution to all your HR problems, but it is a significant tool in your ability to manage risk in your practice.

What's in a job description? The main requirements are:

> Title

> Main purpose

> Reporting lines

> Expected tasks and responsibilities

> Qualifications

> Person specification

> Salary and benefits.

Title: This doesn't need to be all-encompassing but should give some idea of the general role. Be wary of using 'manager', 'director' and other such hierarchical words without any great meaning. Adding numerous layers of hierarchy to your organisation rather negates the title itself.

Main purpose: Be sure that you know why the role exists and what its main purpose is. This should be two or three sentences at most. Focus on what this role does that no other role does and what is expected of it that no other role fulfils.

Reporting lines: Note anyone who reports to this role or anyone who will be expected to be answerable to it. State who this role reports to. It's also worth pointing out whether there is a clear direct management structure or if it's shared. If you get this simple aspect of a job description as clear as you can from the start, you can save hours of explanation and meetings later in the day.

Expected tasks and responsibilities: Break these down into topics (e.g. financial, project management, reporting, people management, design, resourcing). Make sure you list the key elements and expectations (e.g. responsible for monitoring the design output of the team). You aren't expected to list the individual steps by which this aspect of the role would be carried out; you can assume that a person experienced in such a role would be able to work it out for themselves.

Qualifications: Break it down into essential or required, and beneficial. What is really necessary for the role?

Person specification: Be careful with this section. This is probably the most fraught with potential for discrimination. Here you need to avoid stating your requirement for a 'young active candidate who will fit into our mostly female office' or similar. What does the role really need? It is extremely easy to be subjective about personal attributes. You will see many statements on CVs that are effectively meaningless because they are trying to appeal to any requirements: 'Team player who can work on their own and is a demonstrable self-starter.' 'Shows initiative, but responds positively to instruction.' Be careful about seeking someone who 'demonstrates innovation and creativity', but who won't be allowed to show it because the senior designer doesn't let anyone else's ideas out of the door.

Salary and benefits: There is a tendency within many practices to be cagey about their salaries offered and even benefits given. This information does not remain secret for long. Certain companies will be known to pay attractive salaries or offer a well-rounded benefits package. If you simply say 'salary on application' or something similar, you are giving yourself even more work to do in terms of sifting applicants. Also, some guide to the salary level will give a further indication of the level of candidate that you are seeking. It's also important to have realistic expectations that you'll get the person you want for the salary you are offering. If you want some flexibility, put a salary range in the job description: after all, the job description is not an offer or contract of employment so you can offer more or less if you believe that this is appropriate for a particular candidate.

GATES

> These are basic, essential and legitimate requirements of the role. Once you have ensured that they are not in any way discriminatory, you can use them to vet CVs. Quite simply, if the applicant does not demonstrate the skill or knowledge required, they can legitimately be turned down.

> This is a fundamental step towards creating your shortlist. The same can applyto interviews. If you set out certain key skills or characteristics that you wish to see demonstrated and ask

appropriate non-discriminatory questions, you can turn down the candidate if they do not meet these. This is where the time spent creating a job description shows its worth.

3. MANAGING THE RECRUITMENT PROCESS

One of the most common complaints about recruitment is that the process seems to take so long. You'll often find that there is a bottleneck of some sort and this tends to be because the administrative person who is liaising with agencies, collating CVs and sending holding emails to prospective candidates has come up against a brick wall. This is usually related to the availability of the people who are tasked with signing off the job description, deciding the salary and conducting the interviews. Does the senior partner insist on seeing all the CVs, but is then too busy to do so?

It is not generally necessary for a partner or director to liaise with recruitment agencies or read every CV that arrives, but someone with authority or decision-making power does need to be actively involved in the whole process. It will depend upon the size of the company.

Be realistic about who's doing what. A properly briefed administrator can take care of all the routine process tasks, and even carry out a first review of the CVs to weed out those who do not demonstrate the basic 'gates'.

Make times in your diary to focus on the parts of the recruitment process that only you can do:

> Reviewing the remaining CVs and deciding who's worth interviewing – a simple Yes, No, Maybe decision is all that's needed

> As well as setting aside day-time interview slots, identify a couple of evenings to be available for interviews – it is rather unreasonable to expect all candidates to be available during the day, especially if they are working.

4. SOURCES OF CANDIDATES – INTERNAL OR EXTERNAL

There are a number of options available to help you find new staff members:

> Internal sources – if there is someone who can satisfy the needs of the role and is becoming available or could be swapped from another project or team, or who has expressed a desire to learn this role; or by advertising the role internally

> Work experience / students / graduate programme

> Employee referral (of external candidates)

> External advertising

> Recruitment agency

> Headhunter.

EXTERNAL SOURCES

If you decide you need to go outside to source staff, where is it best to go? Here are some of the most common solutions.

Employee referral: This can be incredibly successful because the applicants will already be screened by your employee. They are unlikely to refer someone who is an embarrassment or simply not up to the job. Referral fees reached giddy heights in the days when demand for talent was competitive, but it's worth you investing a few hundred pounds and is an additional employee benefit that works well for both you and your staff. It seems to work best with newer employees. However, despite the positive aspects, there is also the danger that a focus on employee referrals as a recruiting method will mean that you are likely to perpetuate the make-up of your existing workforce, which could result in a gradual limiting of the influx of new ideas and design solutions that would result from a more diverse workforce. In extreme cases, you may inadvertently create a situation of indirect discrimination against under-represented groups.

Other referral: You may gain referred candidates from consultants, suppliers or clients. In this case, it may be politically troublesome if the applicant is unsuccessful and the referee may not be completely clear as to your needs.

Universities: An obvious source of graduates. Establishing links with a university will give you first choice of the best students.

Direct applicant: The number and quality will depend upon the economy and your practice's reputation. This is seen as a cheap method of recruitment, but remember to account for the cost of time to check quality of work and references. You may also attract many overseas applicants who may not have the right to work in the UK without a work permit or similar. Do you want to get involved in such processes?

Your own company website: Again, this will depend upon your reputation, and has the same challenges that direct applicants pose. We'll be discussing the importance of your reputation later in this chapter.

Generic website: On the face of it, using generic websites (e.g. Totaljobs) is a cheap option, but it can be very time consuming in terms of looking through applicants and checking the quality of their work and experience. This is unlikely to be very successful except perhaps for more junior roles or some support staff roles.

🖳 www.totaljobs.com

Professional website: Using an advanced search option in sites such as LinkedIn, with key words to find prospective candidates, is becoming a more prevalent method of conducting a form of search without using an external intermediary. Although this may save you a significant fee, do remember to factor in the time you will need to take to check references and right to work, as well as verifying the content of the individual's profile.

🖳 www.linkedin.com

Focused website: Specialist websites (e.g. AJ, BD, Dezeen) are common sources of candidates, and people on the hunt for jobs will look at these websites regularly. This is a reasonably priced option, but again you will need to put in place a process for reviewing CVs and checking the quality of applicants. The onus will be on you to follow up references and ensure that applicants have the right to work in the UK.

www.architectsjournaljobs.com
www.bd4jobs.com
www.dezeenjobs.com

Recruitment agency: These will vary in quality. Some will work tremendously hard to find candidates that are the best match for your brief; they will meet them, take references, and only put forward candidates that are appropriate. Others will simply send CVs to make up the numbers and do little research about past work or even whether the applicant can work in the UK legitimately. A good test is how many CVs are sent through – if you are inundated, I would suggest there is little quality control or your brief was too generic (e.g. 'I want an architect'). If an agency apologises and says they have not sent through many CVs because they feel that the candidates aren't right for you, I'd say that was a positive factor in their favour.

Headhunter/executive search firm: These have the reputation of being hideously expensive, and in monetary terms this can certainly be the case. However, for senior key roles or very specialist roles, their typically more thorough approach to candidates can work in your favour.

Your choice may be influenced by your budget, but always remember the cost of your time. For instance, headhunters may seem prohibitively expensive, but they do a significant amount of work for their money. They will interview in depth, they will have been properly and fully briefed, they will usually meet all candidates and follow up references. On the other hand, people who apply through your website will have read about your practice, understand the type and quality of work you do, and you may strike it lucky – it could be an easy way to find an amazing talent!

5. JOB ADVERTISEMENTS

A snappy headline draws attention to the advertisement: 'Architect sought' versus 'Highly innovative and quirky design studio seeks keen advocate of team working and flexible working practices, must be a registered architect'. This is the first thing that potential candidates will read and should be used to attract them to read further but also be very clear as to what is important to you. The vaguer or more generic you are, the less likely you are to have suitable applications.

Focus on the essentials: what do you need the person to be able to do? Basic requirements might include:

> Speak English well in order to articulate a brief or design solution

> Demonstrate excellent drawing skills, both by hand and using CAD

> Travel to job sites

> Manage all aspects of a contract.

In particular, avoid making a specific reference to any of the protected characteristics, described in Chapter 2 – The legal bit. The table on the next page highlights some potential pitfalls.

INAPPROPRIATE WORDING	WHAT TO USE INSTEAD
Words such as 'lively', 'vibrant', 'active' – these have potential for disability discrimination	If you mean physically active, be sure that this is a requirement of the role. If this is about personal approach, state that the applicant should have a pro-active approach or an enthusiasm for design.
'Young', 'would suit more mature candidate' – these have potential for age discrimination	Simply state what characteristics you are seeking. You could use 'enthusiastic', or 'should have a considered approach'.
'Must have 10 years' experience' – a phrase that has potential for age discrimination	Think carefully about what this may mean: what might applicants have achieved after 10 years and not 9 or 8 or 5? The key here is what skills you expect candidates to have, so focus on that instead.
Use of 'he', 'she' or gender specific references or images – this would have potential for sex discrimination	Use 'they' or 'you' as alternatives.

When writing the advertisement, don't forget to be as specific as you can about the application procedure. For instance, do you want people to send in CVs or fill out an application form? (An application form can provide more detail than a CV, for instance.) Do you expect candidates to send in a portfolio? If so, how will they do this (email, hard copy?) and how many examples do you want?

It can also be helpful to mention the timetable (closing date, likely interview dates).

🄰 Application form

6. CONSIDERING YOUR OWN REPUTATION

Essentially, you are aiming to be a practice that prospective candidates are aware of and would be interested in joining. This revolves around how your organisation is viewed by the marketplace.

We've talked in earlier chapters about the profession and how the working environment has evolved for architects. Part of that evolution has been a level of self-examination: not only what is the sector in which a practice works, what geographical area is covered, or even what client type is serviced, but also what ethical and cultural values are demonstrated by the work and exemplified by the staff.

The reasons for these developments are complex, and influenced by both social and commercial changes beyond the scope of this book.

It is now commonly expected that companies will have a mission and 'values' – often housed in a statement – articulating the reasons for founding the company and the way in which it does business. This serves as the company's face to the world. Any website, marketing materials, bids for work and PR work project and

RECRUITMENT
FINDING THE APPLICANT EXTERNALLY

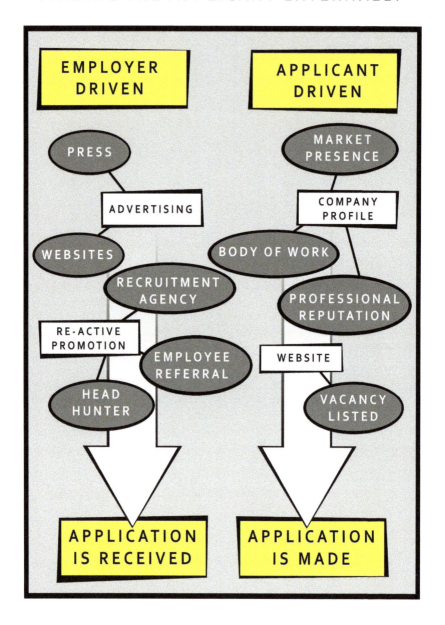

perpetuate this image. In reality, this message may only be skin deep; and it is in the context of HR that the practice's real culture becomes evident. HR acts to reinforce the practice's culture in its policies, procedures and actions. If there is a lack of consistency between the image and reality, it makes HR's role exceedingly difficult, if not impossible, to fulfil. It is also important to remember that people working at the practice will tell their own story which may form the reality, despite any intended image.

As discussed in Chapter 2, recruitment and release are the aspects of the HR lifecycle that interact most obviously with the marketplace. However, professional conduct throughout the employment lifecycle also throws light onto the culture of a company.

This matters because, if you are trying to attract the best and most talented staff, they may be initially attracted by the website and marketing materials, but if they are taking their application seriously they will look further. They will speak to current and former employees; they will make judgements based on how they are treated at interview and how efficient the recruitment process appears; they will assess what the office environment looks like and how people seem to treat each other. Do the words in the mission statement match their experience? If they do not, will you attract candidates who will flourish in your practice or will they be a poor fit and leave?

Now is the time for honest self-examination. Almost without exception, every architecture practice will say that their main driver is design. This may be a goal, but it is clearly not a reality. For some, making a profit is the main aim, with a hope that it can be achieved with a decent level of design; for others, the aim may be functionality, or fulfilling a client request, or specialising in environmentally friendly design, or supporting social needs … or, indeed, design.

So how can you test the reality of your reputation against your original goals?

When you're recruiting, ask yourself why someone would want to work at your practice or company. They may be attracted because you work in a particular sector of design, for a particular client type, by the way you approach design, the way you interact with clients, your amazing career development opportunities and support, or your great benefits package, or the fact that the principal holds mentoring lunches every Friday to talk about architecture and the future of the profession. This is partly about your brand, but it's also about the realities of the practice and what's enjoyable about being there.

Today, any candidate who is worth having will want to know these things. They will also no doubt be attending interviews elsewhere and so will be comparing your practice with others. If you are able to clearly and enthusiastically (and honestly) articulate what your practice is all about this should help you attract the right staff who will stay with you and help you achieve your vision.

Ask yourself these questions:

> Why did I start this practice and what sort of working environment was I trying to create?

> How well have I succeeded?

> Why do I like coming to work and do I know why my staff like coming to work?

> What is our workplace like in terms of physical environment?

> Is it close to public transport (prosaic, I know, but important)?

> What is the dress code?

> What is the reception area or the first space that new candidates see like?

> Is the atmosphere calm or frenzied; quiet or noisy?

> Do we have a real work–life balance or do we treat working through the night as a rite of passage?

> Do we genuinely encourage and support flexible working?

As you examine each of these elements in turn, be honest and seek input from those who will know the true story, such as clients, past employees, current employees, suppliers, or consultants. Themes will emerge. Is the company obsessed with finance or rather careless with money; is there a theme of focus on quality or speed of operation? You can also use tools such as exit interviews (see Chapter 7) or staff and client surveys to add further layers of information.

It is true to say that the partners and senior staff in any company usually believe that they are fully aware of their company's reputation, but this belief is often misplaced. External perception and internal perception can often be very different. I've sat in board rooms listening to directors describing their design-led practice, when in reality their reputation is that of undercutting their competitors to get work. It's therefore very important to use the right tools to seek out answers to these cultural questions. If you ask the wrong people, or ask in the wrong way, you may not receive an honest response and the whole exercise may be futile.

EMAIL RESPONSE TO ALL APPLICANTS

An important part of cultivating a positive reputation (discussed above) is how you communicate with applicants, even those you never meet. Don't join the ranks of practices that don't respond to applicants and gain the reputation of rudeness and arrogance. It is easy to reply to applicants: all you need is a simple email in order to maintain the positive image of your organisation.

EXAMPLE EMAIL TO ALL APPLICANTS

Thank you very much for your application to work at [ABC practice].

Unfortunately, due to the tremendous amount of interest, we will only be able to respond to those applications that we will be taking further. Therefore, if you do not hear from us within the next [two weeks], you can assume that your application has not been successful on this occasion.

We wish you well in your job search.

7. SIFTING APPLICATIONS

This can be a time-consuming activity, but it is important to be as fair as possible in your choice of interviewee (see Chapter 2: The legal bit). Nevertheless it may be tempting to be a little bit ruthless. I'm not suggesting that you should ignore an obviously talented or interesting candidate out of hand. There is a school of thought that you should always try to find a place for an outstanding applicant. But this does rather depend upon budgetary constraints and begs the question whether it would be fair on the individual to hire them if you may not be able to fulfil their career goals and aspirations.

You will probably have asked for a CV and samples of work. I suggest that you limit the samples of work requested to two or three pages of A4 maximum. This should easily give you an idea of the standard and type of work that the candidate can demonstrate. More complete portfolios of work can be brought to an interview. If this simple request is ignored, consider what this tells you about the candidate.

Check the most obvious issues: have they spelt the company name correctly and have they used the correct company name (getting the company name wrong happens when the candidate is making mass applications). Again, what does this sort of carelessness tell you about the candidate?

Next, consider your essential job requirements or 'gates'. Check the educational requirements or qualifications, or language needs, or software skills that are fundamental to the role. If these are not demonstrated, you need a good reason to take the application further. Sort the applications into 'no', 'maybe' and 'yes'. Ensure that rejection emails are sent to the 'no' applicants, if appropriate. Try to be as decisive as possible with the 'maybe' applicants. Often they can get forgotten. If you have only a few 'yes' applicants to interview, perhaps add one or two 'maybes'. But be sure to communicate with all. Even if you reject an applicant at this point, keep their application for a little while, because you can always get back in touch if another more appropriate role arises.

The key things are communication and maintaining the momentum of the process. In particular, when you have made your selection, be sure to explain what the next step is: will it be a conventional interview, will there be a test, should they prepare a presentation.

8. THE SELECTION PROCESS

Despite the plethora of selection methods that now exist, the most commonly used are still the CV/ application form and the interview; usually followed up by reference checking. And yet, the interview process has mixed levels of success.

INTERVIEWS

Here are some golden rules to help you make the best use of the interview process:

> Use the same interviewers as often as you can so that you can more easily compare like with like.

> Be sure that your interviewers have received at least some basic

33

training in questioning techniques so they don't get you into trouble with claims of discrimination. Remember the protected characteristics discussed in Chapter 2.

> Follow the same process with all candidates. You might consider using an interview form to act as a memory jogger and to be sure that your questions are objective and relevant to the role. Again, this helps you to compare candidate information legitimately and also further protects you against claims of discrimination.

> Ask objective, open questions.

🅐 Interview form

INTERVIEW TRAPS

Do any of these approaches seem familiar?

> **Clone hiring: 'oh, they're just like so and so that I know and get on with; I'll hire them.'**

> **Mirror hiring: 'he/she's like me, I like me, I'll hire them....'**

> **Warm body hiring: 'this person is alive and breathing and available and I'm desperate....'**

Getting the interview process right will make your job so much easier.

What can you ask? The simple answer is to use open questions that focus on the candidate's work.

> Quite simply, ask questions that can't just be answered by Yes or No.

> Strike a balance between interrogation and drawing out the candidate.

> Focus on something on their application that indicates an interest and that will start them talking.

> Interject to frame the interview to find out what you need to know about their experience and approach to work.

> Listen.

> Use silence – don't be afraid of it and feel the need to fill gaps.

HOW TO REMEMBER OPEN QUESTIONS

'I keep six honest serving men (they taught me all I knew); their names are What and Why and When and How and Where and Who.'

Rudyard Kipling

RECRUITMENT
THE INTERVIEW PROCESS

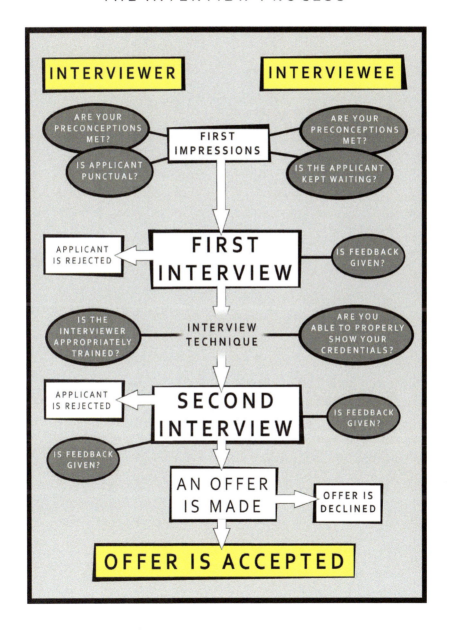

> Use sounds or short words of encouragement: Uh-huh, Go on, I see, Hmmm.

> Restate and reflect feelings from the interviewee. Allow them to expand.

> If you think that the candidate's application may be taken further, you CAN ask them if they have the right to work in the UK. More on this later.

🅐 Interview questions

WHAT NOT TO DO

Avoid references to the protected characteristics (see Chapter 2): age, disability, gender reassignment, marriage and civil partnership, pregnancy and maternity, race, religion or belief, sex, sexual orientation.

Examples of questions that are not work related and so could be challenged:

> How old are you?

> Do you have any plans to have children?

> Are you married?

> How about lunch then?

> What are you doing after this interview?

> What nationality are you? Where were you born?

> Your accent is unusual, is English your first language?

> How's your health? Do you take many sick days?

> Do you have a partner?

OVERHEARD INAPPROPRIATE INTERVIEW COMMENTS ARCHIVE

> 'That's a lovely shirt you're wearing – the colour really suits you.'

> 'What's that perfume? – it's really sexy.'

> 'Are you single? Do you fancy going out?'

> 'Will your husband mind you travelling for work?'

> 'We don't like hiring single mothers because they have loads of time off.'

> 'Part-time workers can't get on here – it just doesn't work in a design practice.'

> 'We like to hire cheap people – it makes our projects more profitable.'

> 'We've got some really attractive men/women in this office – it's great to have something good to look at.'

> 'We cater for all types here – black, white, gay, straight – open house for all sorts.'

Be more creative about how you find out what you want to know. The table opposite lists some questions to be avoided and alternatives to use.

Further pointers: Make sure that you use all your senses and all the information that is available to you, as well as the answers to your questions, to make as full an assessment of the interviewee as you can.

WHAT TO AVOID	CREATIVE SOLUTIONS
'Can you work under pressure?'	Do you really think that a candidate is going to come clean and say: 'Well, no, I completely fall apart if I'm given too many deadlines to achieve; I'd rather work at my own pace'? Try: 'Can you tell me about a time when you were given conflicting project deadlines and how you resolved that?'
'What are your greatest weaknesses?'	You aren't going to receive insightful confessions by asking this tired question. The most you can expect is a response like: 'I'm a perfectionist' or 'I'm always wanting to improve'. How about asking: 'How do you continue your learning? What areas are you focusing on at the moment?'
Any question beginning with, 'If I speak with your current employer …'	A candidate knows this is unlikely to happen and if it did the likelihood is that the only information offered would be dates of employment and title. **See below for some tips on following up references.**
'Where do you see yourself in five years' time?'	Again, unlikely to elicit true confessions. And if the response is: 'In your role', then you've created an uncomfortable conflict situation. You could simply ask: 'What are your career goals?' or 'How do you see your career developing?'
Any question that is mistakenly designed to show a candidate's personality or creativity such as: 'If you were a car, what make would you be?' or 'What's your favourite colour?'	There was a time when this sort of questions was all the rage, but unless you're an expert in translating the response into likely behaviour at work, this is a bit pointless. However, it's fine to ask about hobbies and interests. 'How do you ensure you maintain your work–life balance?' or 'Are there any aspects of your home life that help to reinforce your work life?'
'What was the last book you read?'	You're unlikely to learn anything from this because a well-prepared candidate will simply state the latest design or management tome. They will basically tell you what they think you want them to hear. You could possibly learn something by asking them who their favourite architect is or what their favourite design classic is.
'Can you tell me about a time you did something embarrassing?'	Yes, I have heard this question asked at an interview! How about substituting: 'Have you ever made a mistake at work and what did you do about it?' or 'We've all had occasions when things haven't gone quite right on a project. Can you tell me about a time when this happened for you and how you dealt with it?'

> Did the candidate arrive for the interview on time? If not, is there a justifiable excuse.

> What is their appearance? Dishevelled or smart? Clean or grubby?

> Can you accurately read their body language? How do they sit in the chair? Are they nervous? What else might it mean?

HOW TO CONCLUDE AN INTERVIEW

> Make sure your notes are an accurate record of the interview and you have all the information you need to make a realistic judgement about the candidate.

> Thank them for coming.

> Give a realistic timeframe within which you'll get back to them.

> Even if they are a great candidate, resist the urge to make an offer on the spot. Wait until you've talked to and compared notes with colleagues. Or sleep on it. A verbal offer can be as binding as a written offer.

OTHER SELECTION TECHNIQUES

Work sampling: It is commonplace in design and creative companies for candidates to bring samples of their work to an interview. Your questioning techniques will help to find out if these are samples of their own work. 'What was it that sparked your idea for this design?' 'Where were you when you thought of this concept?'

Group interviews: These are not commonly used in design companies, except perhaps in graduate recruitment programmes, but they can provide incredible insight into how individuals interact with their peers. Group interviews can tell you an awful lot about interpersonal skills, social confidence, articulacy and general politeness. In a team-based environment the more you can learn about these sorts of skills at interview, the more valuable in your final selection.

Psychometric tests: These are perhaps more commonly used for more senior roles. Valid and properly administered, with correct analysis of findings, these tests can provide useful insights into individual candidates for recruitment and, indeed, promotion. However, it's important to remember both sides of the coin: don't use these tests in isolation as the only means of selection; and don't run the tests (and pay the cost) and then ignore the results completely.

Skill tests e.g. CAD: A useful tool for relevant roles, but depends upon the test itself, so be conscious of who's setting it and what you want to know about the applicant's abilities.

Presentations: Often companies will ask candidates to prepare a presentation on a specific topic or on a subject of their own choosing. Make sure that your guidelines for this presentation are clear: timing, use of visual aids, purpose. Is such a presentation appropriate for the role? What are you assessing?

In short, consider the selection method or methods that will give you the most insight into the candidates and that show you the skills more relevant to the role. Be fair in your approach, using the same selection methods for all candidates for the same role. Be objective.

Remember also that candidates can ask to see any interview notes you've written about them!

9. MAKING A DECISION

After the interviewing process is completed there will probably be obvious candidates for rejection, who you can simply email and thank for their interest. For others, there are further considerations, especially if there is a close choice of suitable candidates. Reviewing references can be helpful at this point.

THE VALUE OF SEEKING REFERENCES

Increasingly, it seems that people are adopting the view that the references you receive for new employees aren't worth the paper they're written on. We've all seen the standard form which asks about dates, role, attendance record, timekeeping, quality of work and so on, usually concluding with the million dollar question: 'would you rehire this person?' However, references are still a useful gauge of the suitability of a candidate.

Firstly, take a look at who the applicant has chosen as referees. In an ideal world, you should seek input from the current and next most recent employer. But realistically, in most cases it would be inappropriate to approach the current employer while the candidate is still employed there. So, check that the referees are former employers and, if so, were they the direct manager of the candidate? Or are they peers or workmates? Ideally, you should be approaching the candidate's former direct manager or a partner or director at that company. If not, ask why. Does the referee still work for the company at which they met the candidate? If you

are in any doubt about the value of the referee, see if you can get a reference for the referee.

We can benefit from the fact that the architecture profession is rather mobile and somewhat incestuous. If you ask around among colleagues and fellow architects, someone will know someone who knows the candidate or the referee.

Secondly, try contacting the referee by phone rather than email or letter. These days the most common form of communication is email. However, you can learn so much more in a phone call. Prepare your questions beforehand. They need only be the standard ones: dates of employment; role; projects worked on; quality of work; strengths and weaknesses. But, be aware of the immediate reaction when you introduce yourself and explain that you are calling to seek a reference for such and such a person. Obviously, jot down the factual answers to the questions that you ask, but listen for the tone of voice, hesitancy in answering and also **what isn't said**. End the call by asking if there is anything else that the referee thinks it would be worth telling you about or if they would like to say anything in support of the individual.

When it comes to giving references, it is very important to be accurate and fair.

10. MAKING AN OFFER

Methods of making an offer of employment vary considerably from one company to another. There are those who believe in an informal approach in the first instance; perhaps a phone call by one of the interviewers giving the basic details of the offer. However, as mentioned earlier, a verbal offer can be as binding as a written offer. Even if you make an offer over the phone, which you later retract, you may find yourself having to pay a sum of money in compensation to the individual. (This is based upon the amount usually paid in notice during a probationary period.)

An offer via email can be considered as formal as a written hard copy contract these days. It may be as well to have the courage of your convictions and make a written offer in the first instance. Certainly email can be used, but follow it up with a good old-fashioned hard copy in the post. Your offer letter can be quite brief, giving the basic package information: salary, benefits, any additional remuneration such as bonuses and holidays, as well as the role and potential start date. If this whets their appetite and they accept your initial offer, you can confirm via email and prepare for their arrival.

At this stage, if you have not already done so, you should ask the potential new hire if they have the right to work in the UK.

PROOF OF RIGHT TO WORK IN THE UK

It is part of your obligation as an employer to ensure that all of your employees have the right to work in the UK and to maintain up-to-date records showing this. If you fail to do so, you may be fined or at worst receive a custodial sentence. In most cases, your new staff member can show you a UK or EEA passport. If they are unable to do

so, you must ask for proof that they have the right to work in the UK on some other basis (e.g. a work permit).

If your new employee cannot provide any of these documents, they cannot work for you and your offer of employment to them should be retracted. The sooner you know this the better. Presumably, if they do not have right to work, they will not accept your offer, but you can't be sure of that.

They should bring the original documents proving their right to work and show them to you on their first day of employment – before they start work.

The subject of immigration is rather too complex to be discussed at length in this context, but see also 'What do you need to see on their first day?' for your administrative obligations.

INDUCTION

Onboarding, orientation, induction – it doesn't matter what you call it, it's all about how a new employee is welcomed to your company and how they become an effective and efficient member of staff as soon as possible.

You may think that an induction is not necessary in a smaller company because you can just help the new staff member settle in as you go along. You may feel it's too formal to have an induction because it doesn't suit the culture of the company. Or you may feel you don't have time to devote to these admin issues because you need the new person working hard on your project immediately. But I advise you to read the salutary lesson below.

BEFORE THEY START

Use this valuable time before your new recruit begins work not only to get ahead with some of the necessary paperwork, but also to educate your new staff member about your company and you. Help them to have realistic expectations. As appropriate, you can provide the following.

Written offer of employment: As we've discussed, your offer doesn't have to be in writing, but it clarifies what you are offering in case there is any doubt or confusion. Your initial verbal offer may have only mentioned salary, but now you can clarify other issues such as holidays, sick leave, payment of professional fees, any additional attractions such as healthcare or gym membership. This can be in the form of a simple letter. You could also clarify the start date and time, who they should ask for, what they need to bring with them (which should include proof of their right to work in the UK). Ask them to write or email to confirm they accept the offer.

CASE STUDY:
A salutary lesson

A senior architect was hired at some expense via a headhunter/ recruitment agency.

On the architect's first day he turned up at the new office but found that he was not expected, his contact was on holiday, and no work had been planned for him. A desk was found and he was set to filing drawings while others rushed to fulfil a deadline. A patient man, he filed drawings for a week, while he listened and learned.

On the Friday afternoon of his first week, he approached the project leader and asked if there was any way he could help. He explained his experience and background. He was told that it was too late to involve him in the project. A disillusioned man, he thought long and hard over the weekend, but his original enthusiasm and impression were damaged beyond repair. He resigned on the Monday.

The headhunter presented an invoice for a finder's fee and pursued payment successfully through the Small Claims Court. The senior architect's friend, who was also being courted by the same company, turned down their offer of employment and went elsewhere because he heard of the unprofessional and disorganised way his friend had been treated.

Yes. This is a true story.

Contract of employment: You need to provide 'written particulars of employment' (see next column) within the first eight weeks of someone's start date. This could be a simple letter covering the necessary issues, or it could be a more lengthy complex document such as a contract of employment. If you provide it before someone starts work, it simply means that they can review the information and any questions can be promptly answered.

Job description: Should I use the word Marmite here? Some people love job descriptions because they provide clarity of expectation; others hate them because they seem to be restrictive. In reality, they are an incredibly versatile management tool, as subsequent chapters will show. I'd suggest using one, however abbreviated. Ideally, you will have created such a thing during your recruitment process, but if not now is the time to do so. We've discussed the contents of a job description earlier in this chapter. It is not technically a legal requirement to provide a job description, but an employee does need to know what their job title or role is. The greater the clarity on your part, as early as possible, the better both you and your new employee will understand all aspects of their employment, including appraisal, reward, recognition and performance management.

Employee handbook: Provide this, if you have one, or a collection of the company's most important policies and procedures.

Practice literature: This could be in the form of literature or perhaps a DVD of your key work which helps to articulate your culture and values. You could also supply a company structure diagram showing key individuals and their roles. An internal telephone directory could be useful, together with any information you may have on the organisation of projects, filing standards and drawing standards. All these provide a level of reassurance for the new employee before their first day.

WRITTEN PARTICULARS OF EMPLOYMENT

> **Name of employer**

> **Name of employee**

> **Start date/date of commencement of continuous employment**

> **Job title or role**

> **Location of work**

> **Salary and when paid**

> **Holiday allowance**

> **Notice period**

> **Sick leave and policy for informing**

> **Disciplinary procedure**

> **Who to go to with any grievance**

> **Details of any trade union agreements**

> **Details of any pension arrangements**

It can be particularly useful, especially if you do not often recruit new staff, to use a checklist for induction to make sure that nothing is overlooked, and to develop a list of basic personal information about staff members for ease of administration and in case of emergencies.

🅐 Induction checklist
🅐 Interview form
🅐 Personal details form

WHAT DO YOU NEED TO SEE ON THEIR FIRST DAY?

Proof of right to work in the UK: This will generally be a UK or EU passport. You need to see an original document; a photocopy is not sufficient. If the situation is less simple (e.g. involving a work permit) you do still need to check the original documents. You are not expected to be an immigration expert, simply use your common sense:

> Check that the photograph and date of birth seem to genuinely relate to your new employee in terms of gender and birth.

> Check that the document does not seem to have been tampered with. I have known a date of birth to be amended in ballpoint pen. (On that occasion, an attempt to seem younger, but nevertheless, illegal.)

> Read any stamps in a passport and ensure they allow the person to work in the UK (e.g. they do not say 'Forbidden from taking employment' or similar).

> Work permits tend to need additional documentation to back them up. You need to see these original documents too.

> Photocopy the cover and the photo details page of the passport, along with copies of all other related documents, for the individual's personnel file. UKVI (UK Visas and Immigration) require that each photocopy be verified, preferably by the same person for all employees. Verification means that you should sign and print your name on the copy, and date it.

> Keep the copies in the employee's personnel file.

If in doubt, seek professional support. You can seek basic advice from the relevant government website. However, the information is notoriously unclear, so you may find it less frustrating and less costly in terms of time to speak to an immigration lawyer.

🕮 www.gov.uk/government/organisations/uk-visas-and-immigration

P45: This is not a legal requirement, but it is an advantage for the new employee if their tax details are known as soon as possible.

Bank details: Again, not a legal requirement, but an advantage for the employee if these are known as soon as possible for payroll purposes.

Contract of employment (or 'Written particulars of employment'): Although these do not have to be given to the employee to sign immediately, providing it early means that any problems or queries can be addressed as soon possible. Go through the basics of the contract and ask the new employee to sign two copies; one for your records and one for their own.

HOW TO MANAGE THE ORIENTATION

Allocate a 'buddy': Appoint a person to show your new recruit to their workstation and introduce them to colleagues, and to explain more informal aspects such as local sandwich bar, social activities.

Employ other members of staff: Encourage other colleagues to undertake the part of the induction relevant to their work area. In this way, the new employee meets more than one person and knows who to go to for specific specialist information:

> IT – allocate login details, explain the network structure and any key IT policies

> Marketing – key projects and clients; explanation of how the company presents itself at networking events

> HR – key policies or employee handbook, appraisal system

> Finance – payroll, protocols for expenses, benefits

> Office administrator – filing standards, template documents

> Director – history of the company, mission and values

> Health and safety – this can be undertaken by a health and safety representative if there is one, but even if there isn't, it is important that this aspect is covered (typically, by HR) – fire safety, first aid, any particular hazards

> Manager/team leader – CAD standards, project brief.

SUMMARY: THE VALUE OF RECRUITMENT

It is almost impossible to exaggerate how important it is to get the recruitment process right. Time, thought and preparation at this stage will save you so much time, money, anxiety, low morale, conflict, damage to reputation and project impact later in the day.

At the risk of sounding repetitive, take the time to plan your process and engage your staff in ensuring that only the right people join you. Remember the salutary lesson!

> Really think about your current needs and future requirements.

> Remember the importance of career development to your existing staff and give them a chance to fill a need if possible.

> Write a job description for your own and the candidate's benefit.

> Remember your own reputation and consider the process that the candidates will experience when they apply to your company.

> Always remember your need to comply with legal requirements.

REWARD

Now that you've enticed the most talented candidates to join your company, you will need to give significant thought to how you are going to reward them for their hard work.

This chapter will focus on:

> Defining reward and what it means in your company

> Ideas for financial and non-financial rewards

> Being clear about what you want to reward.

1. DEFINING REWARD: WHAT IT IS, OR SHOULD BE

We need to begin with an attempt to distinguish between 'reward' and 'recognition'.

To some, the word 'reward' automatically means money. But if you ponder on it for a little longer, the reality is rather more complex. There is a plethora of other things that a company can offer to staff which come under the umbrella of 'reward'. And, let's face it, if a creative company can come up with innovative solutions for its clients, it should be able to do the same for its people!

REWARD VERSUS RECOGNITION – THE DIFFERENCE

> Reward and recognition are often mentioned in tandem. In reality, reward is a form of recognition. However, for the

purposes of this book,
I am focusing on reward as a tangible thing – incorporating both financial and non-financial elements, but ultimately something that can be quantified or measured.

> We will discuss recognition in Chapter 6, from the perspective of recognition in the broadest sense of acknowledgement – ranging from some kind of award or title or opportunity, to a simple thank you for a job well done.

Superficially, this topic is most influenced by the dynamics of company size and profitability. There is an expectation that larger companies will have more money to allocate to salaries and remuneration packages. However, this may not always be the case. We can all think of some of the smaller boutique companies who wish to stay that way but still have the ability to pay above-average salaries and other monetary rewards.

Also, as we shall discuss later in this chapter, smaller companies have certain characteristics which give them advantages over larger companies. It's a question of finding the reward package that suits the individuals in your organisation.

REWARD IS NOT

> A dinosaur award for long service

> A sop for someone who isn't good enough to be promoted

> A silencer for the person who shouts the loudest

> A bonus for just turning up to work

> A prize for bad behaviour

> An incentive for someone who is performing badly to continue to do so.

You also need to take into account the increasing focus on the individual in the workplace.

Generic reward systems may be fairer and easier to administrate, but more personal reward systems may be more effective. Given this contradiction, it seems sensible to start with some commonly held ground rules:

> Not everyone is motivated by money, but if you see your peers earning more, you will be disgruntled.

> Different rewards will be better received at different stages of your life or career. This is where understanding the individuals in your company will reap its own rewards. Take a look at the demographics of your staff.

> Don't just throw money at it. Take into account what other resources you may have available to you. All companies of whatever size and composition will have different things to offer.

> You need to be fair about what is offered. In simple terms, offer the same benefits in monetary value to all staff or structure your reward

THE CHANGING APPROACH TO REWARD

systems so that it is transparent and different levels are clearly defined and against clear non-discriminatory criteria. (Remember the legal bit, from Chapter 2?)

> Try to offer a range of rewards – financial and non-financial. Some examples are given in the table below.

A reward plan in place must be based on research:

> Benchmark salaries – there are lots of useful websites (see below). Recruitment agencies also have up-to-date information, especially those that specialise in your specific creative area.

> Look at what your competitors do. Speak to people you know in the industry and ask those who you've recently hired about their former employers.

> Find out what interests your staff have and come up with rewards that will reflect these. They may be work- or home-orientated.

> Take a look at companies that you admire and what they offer to their

EXAMPLES OF REWARDS AND BENEFITS	SUITABILITY AND VALUE HELD
Bonus	All staff – pays off credit cards or contributes to savings plan.
Private healthcare	Typically favoured by more mature staff members or those with a health condition, although pre-existing conditions may not be covered under basic healthcare schemes; if dependants are also covered by the company scheme, those with children will also find this a positive reward.
Life insurance	Valued by those with dependants.
PHI (permanent health insurance), income protection, long-term disability insurance	Typically of less value to younger, healthier employees.
Gym membership	Valued by all, but typically of more value to younger employees.
Cycle to Work vouchers	Clearly of value to those who like cycling or who are able to cycle to and from work.
Childcare vouchers	Of value to those with children!
Study days	Those at the beginning of their career or undergoing a change in direction.
Additional holiday	Appreciated by all. (Except the office martyr who cannot be spared from their work – every company has one.)
Leaves of absence/sabbaticals	Valued by all, but particularly valued by those who have a project they wish to fulfil or who are working away from their home country.

CASE STUDY:
Tailoring the reward structure to the demographics of the company

A few years ago, I became aware of a recruitment company who gave their employees six months' leave of absence at full pay after every five years of employment.

Why so generous you may wonder? Because the vast majority of the employees were from Australia or New Zealand. Six months off gave them time to visit home and reconnect with family and friends, but the generous terms commanded their loyalty to return to work at the end of the leave.

It worked well, retention was high and turnover low.

staff. This may better reflect the culture you are hoping to develop and maintain.

> Seek input from your staff. You may be aware of their interests, but only they can tell you what their current priorities in life are.

> Remember that it doesn't actually have to be financial. Smaller businesses may perhaps have less cash to utilise in this way, but have other things to offer.

📖 www.ribaappointments.com/Salary-Guide.aspx

HOW TO AVOID DISCRIMINATION IN YOUR REWARD SYSTEM

Length of service: Be careful that this does not inadvertently favour older members of staff. Keep it to rewarding a maximum of ten years' service.

Part-time staff: Offer proportionate benefits depending on the number of hours worked. If you can't do so, err on the side of caution and offer the full benefit.

Rewards that recognise out of hours work or extra-curricular activities that only take place on certain days may also be discriminatory against part-time workers and potentially indirectly discriminatory against women, so be careful with this!

Fixed-term staff: Should be offered the same benefits as permanent staff.

Agency workers: May be entitled to some benefits after 12 weeks' service.

ADVANCED REWARD

Flexible benefits exist but are most common in the larger organisations because they can be complex and take up significant administrative time, or require robust technology standards in the instance of employee self-management. They can also be known as 'cafeteria benefits' or 'flex plans'. I've even heard them described as a 'buffet of benefits'. You get the general idea – there is an element of personal choice on the part of the employee: they can vary their pay and benefits to suit individual personal requirements.

In simple terms, this may mean that employees can either retain their existing basic salary while varying the mix or levels of various benefits, or they can adjust their salary up or down by taking fewer or more benefits respectively. So, the dividing line between pay and benefits is less rigid than in standard reward systems.

2. IDEAS FOR FINANCIAL AND NON-FINANCIAL REWARDS

To clarify, here is what you **must** offer your employees:

> **A salary or pay**: Financial compensation in return for work. A minimum wage does apply.

> **28 days' paid holiday**: Most workers who work a five-day week must receive 28 days' paid annual leave per year. This may include bank holidays. This is linked to the Working Time Directive which also governs hours of work per day and week, rest periods, night working and various other stipulations.

> **Various statutory leaves**: These include maternity, paternity, parental, adoption, shared parental, dependant care, and others, and may or may not have statutory pay associated with them.

> **Statutory sick pay**: This has pretty specific rules about how it works and it is best to check the government websites for up-to-date information.

> **Time off for jury service and various other commitments**: Jury service can be deferred so long as the appropriate procedure is followed. Other commitments include a wide range of activities such as trade union duties, antenatal appointments, and also time off under the Working Time Directive.

You do not have to offer bonuses or other financial rewards, or additional holiday for long service, or additional sick leave.

A NOTE ABOUT UNPAID INTERNSHIPS

> **This is a subject that has attracted a fair amount of debate, but the salient point is that there is a world of difference between a couple of weeks' work experience while at school and several months' unpaid work at any other time. Currently, there is a push towards making unpaid internships longer than four weeks illegal. This may have a significant impact on the resourcing for more attractive careers such as the media.**

FINANCIAL REWARDS

These can be broken down into what we can call **traditional** and **innovative**.

There is a school of thought that it should be reward enough to work in an environment that enables you to express your creativity. It is almost as if creativity is a calling or vocation. The old-fashioned image of a painter slaving away in his garret comes to mind.

The current reality is different. Creative companies do not have to sacrifice

REWARD

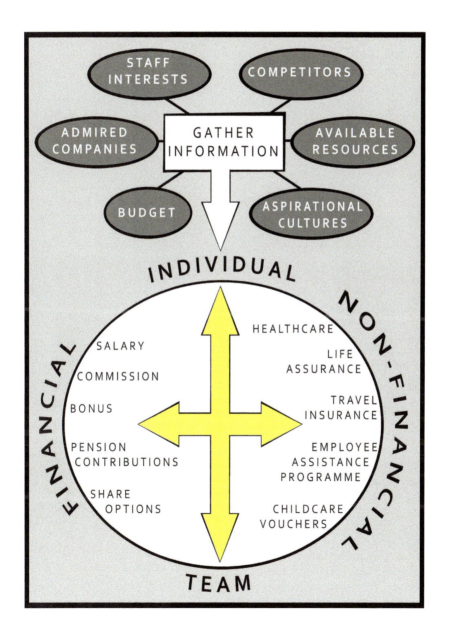

STAFF INTERESTS

COMPETITORS

ADMIRED COMPANIES

GATHER INFORMATION

AVAILABLE RESOURCES

BUDGET

ASPIRATIONAL CULTURES

INDIVIDUAL

NON-FINANCIAL

FINANCIAL

SALARY

COMMISSION

BONUS

PENSION CONTRIBUTIONS

SHARE OPTIONS

HEALTHCARE

LIFE ASSURANCE

TRAVEL INSURANCE

EMPLOYEE ASSISTANCE PROGRAMME

CHILDCARE VOUCHERS

TEAM

commerciality to succeed; nor does commercial success mean that creativity needs to be compromised.

Part of this development is a recognition that talent has a value. If you do not offer appropriate rewards you will either not attract people in the first place or you will eventually lose the people that you already have.

How you address this requires a basic understanding of reward and how it works.

Let's define reward, then, as the tangible benefits that your staff receive in return for their work for your organisation. This can be made up from different building blocks, as follows.

Basic salary: This is the guaranteed 'take home pay'. It is written in the offer letter or contract of employment or whatever other means you have used. It is also the means by which external bodies such as banks and building societies will determine the income of an individual.

Additional variable or non-guaranteed monetary income: There are common examples of this, but they are perhaps less widely explored in creative companies than in other industry sectors:

> **Overtime**: It is not unusual to see clauses in contracts of employment that say something along the lines of 'It is expected that you will work such necessary reasonable additional hours to complete your tasks without additional remuneration'. In essence, you need to finish the work we expect

of you regardless of how long it takes and without any extra pay. This goes back to the idea of creativity as a calling – apparently, you won't mind labouring away for twelve hours a day for a low salary because you will have the personal joy of having created a ... building, interior space, piece of music, computer game, short story ... just fill in the blanks. You can make all sorts of rules about how you'll pay overtime, if you choose to pay it. It is rare to see use of a simple hourly rate multiple based on annual salary (the sort of arrangement that seems to be the norm when you call out a plumber for an emergency or at the weekend). More likely, you could have an arrangement that pays only after a certain number of hours per day have been worked. The main point is to have some kind of structure and stick to it, to avoid favouritism and inconsistency.

> **Bonus**: Occasionally, creative companies will pay a bonus. The most common timeframe for this would be annually. Its payment will obviously be based upon what money is available. The amount may vary, but should be based on some equitable structure – a percentage of salary perhaps. And if you do pay bonuses, be sure to be on firm ground if you choose not to pay bonuses to some people. Can you show an objective reason for doing so? Make certain you have documented any failure to achieve targets or any performance issues. See Chapter 7 for more on performance management.

> **Share options/profit sharing**: This used to be the domain of more senior staff, but is increasingly

used to form a more inclusive reward structure throughout the company. Smaller organisations may dismiss this idea thinking it is perhaps better suited to larger organisations, but I would urge you to seek financial advice about it since it is a great way of engaging your staff and making them feel genuinely a part of the business and its future.

> **Commission**: It is rare for a commission structure to be in place for the majority of staff in a creative company, but worth mentioning for the exceptions. For example, a commission structure may be applied to someone charged with obtaining new business. Typically they may receive a lower basic salary with the opportunity for higher monetary gain if they reach certain new business targets. You need to be aware of the likelihood of challenge if paying commission in addition to a regular salary to only a few staff members – you may find yourself with a revolt on your hands from those who say it's unfair on those who don't have the opportunity to gain commission.

Pension/retirement planning: If you have managed to avoid hearing about auto-enrolment – even if you have no idea what it is – you must have been living in a cave since the start of the 2010s. Basically under the Pensions Act 2008, every employer, however small, needs to make pension contributions for their employees. The process of auto-enrolment is, as it suggests, automatic. Every employee will be automatically enrolled into their employer's pension scheme upon the first day of their employment. Setting up a scheme is a specialist area and you should seek advice from an independent financial adviser sooner rather than later. This process takes longer than a few days or weeks to set up. Suffice to say, it will involve internal administration time and is therefore a cost. In addition, you will have to make pension contributions as an employer.

Standard benefits: As it suggests these are put in place for all staff members unless they specifically request not to be included. This happens occasionally if someone feels any tax burden may be too great or perhaps they prefer to support the NHS rather than private healthcare.

Options include:

> Private healthcare – whether just for the employee or for family and dependants too

> Life assurance – multiple of salary given on death may vary according to seniority

> Travel insurance – especially if employee travels regularly for work, could add family as an additional benefit

> Employee assistance programme (EAP) – a reasonably priced option providing a wide range of support services from counselling to legal and financial advice

> Concierge services – OK, so this isn't very common and can be quite expensive, but it's a great idea. Someone to wait in for deliveries, or for tradesmen, or to do your shopping, or any amount of other services. May be provided alongside an EAP.

Flexible benefits: These are available for all staff members, but they should actively opt to take them up if they wish to do so. Obviously, for example, childcare vouchers will not be of interest to everyone:

> Childcare vouchers – a government scheme aimed to save you tax on the cost of childcare

> Cycle to Work scheme – another government scheme enabling employers to loan cycles and cyclists' safety equipment to employees as a tax-free benefit

> Gym membership – could be paid fully or in part by company

> Yoga/neck massage/meditation – classes held in office or local venue paid for by company

> Various discount vouchers – often employers are able to offer various discounted vouchers for shopping or experiences (they are able to do so on the basis of bulk discounts).

Discretionary benefits: Offered by the employer for specific reasons. These can either be for all staff, teams or individuals.

All staff:
> Christmas/annual party

> Annual trip – weekend away to location in the UK or European capital

> Summer family party – picnic with games or elaborate barbecue with music.

Teams/all staff:
> Money behind the bar at local pub – always being conscious of not leaving out those who do not feel comfortable in a pub or who don't drink alcohol

> Meal at good restaurant

> Theatre/film

> Outing to place of interest or exhibition.

Individual:
> Red letter days/vouchers, perhaps to celebrate landmark birthdays or for length of service

> Dinner tickets/days out, to reflect a particular success or contribution by an employee, usually to reflect their love of fine dining, or travel, or theatre or whatever

> Garden centre vouchers/book tokens/spa treatment/personal shopping experience/wine voucher

> Eurostar/budget airline tickets

> Luxury weekend in the UK.

REWARD IN SMALL BUSINESSES

Just because you don't have a lot of cash to flash doesn't mean you can't reward your loyal and hard-working staff. List what resources you have. For instance, does your work environment lend itself to informal mentoring or coaching; does your project structure lend itself to allowing someone to learn on the job rather than sending them on expensive training courses; can you involve people in an initiative that will enhance your working practices, or involve them in presenting designs or projects, or include them in awards or industry events?

In fact, when you add it all up, you may have certain advantages over your larger competitors (see table opposite).

ADVANTAGE	RELATED REWARD/S
Proximity Smaller companies are likely to be in one space with staff working adjacent to each other.	• You can act as coach and mentor to your staff as you work, without complex programmes being developed and extra time being taken out of your busy day.
Communication Should be eased and less contrived because of the proximity. You are likely to know each other better and good communication should be more natural and in the usual course of events.	• Use staff meetings as an opportunity to share and pass on information as a team. • Develop a newsletter to combine work and fun, and to acknowledge individual and team success. • Collaborate on articles or applying for awards. • Social activities such as company paid meals or trips, family days, summer parties, film club, museum or exhibition visits, site visits. • These may not seem obvious rewards, but they are more meaningful because of the time and effort committed by the company.
Time Has some cost of course, but is available as a manageable resource.	• This is partly about time as a reward in terms of offering flexible hours, study leave, more holiday, or the opportunity to work from home occasionally. It is also about using your time to coach and mentor your staff in a more structured way during working hours. Time spent imparting your hard-earned wisdom is invaluable. • Smaller companies do tend to offer greater flexibility of working than larger ones.
Project opportunity So often in larger companies, you can end up in a silo or a pigeon hole. Few people want to spend years of their life detailing door knobs or specifying conference room chairs. So, make positive use of the need for everyone to be rather more multi-skilled in your smaller company. Make a virtue out of necessity.	• Staff may benefit from the opportunity to experience all stages of a project; to follow their chosen career path through a new project type or a new role on a project; and to take on a new experience or face a challenge in a safe environment with you there to help. • Once again, your greater proximity will help here: the risk of potential damage to your projects is minimised because you are there to keep an eye out. • What do staff want to learn? How can their work help them to develop?
Involvement/inclusion Many sources will tell you that this will appeal to your Generation Y staff members particularly.	• Internal initiatives – study groups, mentoring, technology workshops, working together to improve drawing standards or sorting out the resourcing library. • External initiatives – foster involvement in social, charitable, community, sustainability projects. • Business strategy and planning – seek input and feedback from your team on certain aspects. • This will help to satisfy a need for inclusion and involvement.

continued overleaf ⋯⋗

Acknowledgement/ contribution	• Put a thank you on your noticeboard or intranet or even your website.
The contribution that individuals make within a small company tends to be rather more obvious than in larger companies where a manager could perhaps take the credit for a team member's work.	• Mention the incident or event at a staff meeting – this may seem unduly formal for a small company, but try to do something beyond hollering across the office about it. • Suggest that the individual leads an initiative, is the go to person for a particular field of expertise, or is the recognised office expert in a particular area.

Never forget the importance of the social aspects of work. A few hundred pounds spent on a meal or company outing will generally be well spent. However, do be sure that you aren't inadvertently excluding anyone (e.g. if it's drinks at the pub, is there anyone who would be uncomfortable in a pub or around alcohol?).

Just remember what you can do so much better than many larger organisations:

> Know your staff

> Use your advantages: ease of communication, opportunities for inclusion, experience as generalists rather than specialists, learning opportunities through proximity, flexibility of working practices.

3. BEING CLEAR ABOUT WHAT YOU WANT TO REWARD

You are always going to be pulled in at least two different directions when you're managing people in a creative environment. Creativity suggests flexibility; HR suggests rules and regulations. However, remember that in Chapter 2 when discussing what HR can be to a company, we talked about HR as an enabler? Here's a pertinent metaphor:

> HR can provide the trampoline that will enable you to reach ever greater heights of creativity.

Have you ever read *Orbiting the Giant Hairball* by Gordon MacKenzie? It discusses the possibility that truly creative people can benefit from some element of structure or foundation in order to be so. So, a structure is not all bad, and will also enable you to address more effectively any people-related problems that may arise.

In effect, you need to start with the concept of giving like reward for like roles. If there is any inconsistency

Job Role	20	25	30	35	40	45	50	55	60	65	70	75	80	85	90	95	100	105	110
Project Director									■	■	■	■	■	■	■	■	■	■	■
Design Manager				■	■														
Senior Architect						■	■	■											
Intermediate Designer			■																
Project Architect						■	■	■											
Architect			■	■															
Interior Designer		■																	
Part II		■																	
Junior Designer	■																		
Graduate	■																		
Salary (£'000s)	20	25	30	35	40	45	50	55	60	65	70	75	80	85	90	95	100	105	110

or differentiation, you need to have a good reason or reasons for doing so. At the risk of sounding like a broken record, this is where the job description is invaluable. Clearly, people on the same grade or with the same job title may not have exactly the same job description. If they don't, this is one means of differentiating and perhaps enabling flexibility in pay or reward. However, it is essential to be clear about what is/isn't subject to reward.

Let's take the steps in turn:

1. Start from the premise that each job title will have a general pay range, as illustrated in the diagram [above]. This is very generic so do not use it as a guide for plotting your salaries! Obviously salaries will be influenced by location, years of experience, and so on, but you will be able to create some general ranges within which to work.

2. Examine the related job descriptions for any differences or increased responsibility or tasks. Highlight these against each individual.

3. Plot individuals on your salary banding diagram or a similar visual aid. It's then much easier to see the differences and determine whether they are justified.

4. Consider your company culture and what behaviour and attitudes you are trying to engender. Pinpoint examples of behaviour and attitudes that have been demonstrated by your staff (discussed in more detail at the end of this chapter). These are potential reasons for reward above and beyond the basic structure.

You can develop your standard reward structure around salary, financial and non-financial benefits as set down in your contract of employment. You then have the opportunity to offer discretionary rewards to those who have acted above and beyond the role for which they were hired.

WHAT IS IT THAT YOU WANT TO SEE FROM YOUR STAFF?

Some things are quite simple and obvious, and may well have cropped up in the original advertisement for the job. Nevertheless, it is important to consider whether your expectations are reasonable, and what factors are essential.

Timekeeping: This has to be essential, doesn't it? If someone can't be on time for work, what hope is there of them being on time with project deadlines?

Reliability: If you never know whether they are going to deliver or what attitude they are going to demonstrate on any given day, how will they conduct themselves in front of clients?

Positive attitude: They may be amazing at their work, but if they are constantly moaning or expressing negative views about the company, their work, you, or the team, could

they be trusted to represent the company positively and demonstrate your company's ethos in front of a client?

Good interpersonal skills: As it used to say on your school report, do they 'play well with others'? In creative environments, legend has it that everyone is a diva. That's not to say we haven't all seen examples of such diva-esque behaviour on occasion, but it is more commonly recognised that selfish, attention-seeking behaviour is not the way to get on in the world, let alone at work.

The above factors should all be essential and, if they are not demonstrated, should be addressed. It is not easy to reduce the basic rewards due to an individual as set out in their contract of employment, but it is possible if you follow due process (see Chapter 7).

However, pause for a moment and remind yourself that what we are considering here is how to reward those who have gone **above and beyond** your expectations. What have they done? How have they behaved? Why is this good? You need to seek examples of these actions or behaviours so that you can reward them specifically, and hopefully engender a virtuous circle of repeated behaviour or actions. The idea is that if other staff members see these things being rewarded they will do them too.

TYPE OF CULTURE	TYPICAL CHARACTERISTICS	SUGGESTED REWARD IDEAS OR THEMES
Collegiate and team orientated	Strong interpersonal skills throughout; strong social culture.	Team activities – outings; team building exercises; group initiatives; team development.
Intellectually challenging and erudite	Cutting edge skills development, encouragement of debate.	Organised opportunities to enhance knowledge such as: attendance at lectures to gain new ideas; subscription to publications and journals; exploring academic theory via research or speakers; support for research and study.
Dynamic and innovative	Loose structure, greater flexibility and a focus on individualism; open to change; supportive of risk. and new ways of working.	Focus on new experiences: days away, trips, more paid time off to experience new cultures; response to individual's particular interests (e.g. ballooning, sky diving).

Examples include:

> Project contribution in terms of focused hours or specific skill or additional know-how

> Mentoring team members and passing on own expertise and knowledge

> Volunteering for extra-curricular activities such as training or interviewing

> Contributing towards the general feeling of staff wellbeing – may be positive attitude, or bringing in cakes, or making tea, or supporting a team member who is upset or under pressure.

Some ideas to create a reward structure that echoes your company culture and is unique to you are listed in the table above.

Consider the following situation: your team includes two qualified architects, each with eight years' experience. One arrives at work on time, gets on with the work, meets deadlines, and produces work of a good standard. The other does exactly the same, but also mentors junior staff during the course of the day, and helps out with interviewing at lunchtimes. So, here you have concrete ways in which you can differentiate between two individuals with a similar job title. One might be at the middle of the pay range; the other higher up.

Also, it may be easy to spot positive things to reward, but you should also be clear about what you don't want to reward.

PRACTICAL ADVICE:
Should you reward overtime?

It is often the case that overtime is worked in creative companies. We tend to be deadline driven and also, you never know when the creative muse might strike and you have to work with it. But, is it always good and to be rewarded?

You have a responsibility to monitor workloads and be reasonable about expectations. Rewarding staff who work overtime simply because they can is unfair on those who can't and in any case will ultimately burn out your staff. I would question the quality of work and ideas produced at three o'clock in the morning under the influence of a bucketful of black coffee.

When considering reward for overtime, look for the following:

Reward if the overtime was:
> Specifically requested by management to help with a one-off deadline

> Specifically requested by management while additional resource is sought

> Volunteered to help out on a short-term basis while additional resource is sought

> Volunteered to help out on a short-term basis because additional resource is unavailable.

Don't reward if the overtime was:
> Worked because saving up for a house/holiday

> Worked because poor at planning workload

> Worked because they think they can store up extra holiday or time off in lieu

> Worked because no one has noticed they are struggling with workload/tasks

> Worked because of lack of training.

Here are some examples of behaviours to be aware of.

Positives:

> Has a positive attitude to work and colleagues

> Willingly helps out other team members

> Occasionally works overtime or longer hours when required

> Demonstrates good timekeeping

> Is reliable

> Is willing to learn.

Negatives:

> Regularly works all night, seems to enjoy sleeping under desk

> Always working overtime even though tasks are not onerous

> Tells you they need help just before missing a deadline

> Always playing the martyr – 'I'm fine, I'll be OK', when clearly not

> Never misses a deadline, but runs their team into the ground to do so

> Exudes negativity and exemplifies the Eeyore syndrome

> Given to histrionics in the workplace

> Willing, but always flustered and disorganised, can never find anything at workstation. The untidy desk does not indicate a creative mind in this instance.

On the other hand, you may well be aware of an HR truism that 5 per cent of your employees seem to take up 95 per cent of your management time. Don't overlook those who keep their head below the parapet when considering rewards.

Some of my examples above may seem a little unfair, but so is penalising someone who can't work overtime because they have childcare responsibilities, and rewarding someone who does overtime regularly because they are so bad at planning their workload.

Similarly, there is a difference between someone who you know is overloaded with work and has to work overtime while you try to source someone to help, and the person who works overtime because they do not get on with the work when they need to.

We can use overtime as an example to show how you can approach reward.

SUMMARY: CREATING A REWARD STRUCTURE

> A reward structure does not need to be complicated.

> The structure needs to be fair and transparent.

> You need to know what you are rewarding and say so.

> You do not need a bottomless pit of financial resources. Use whatever resources you have.

> Be aware of what makes your company unique and focus on that.

> Know your staff and what kind
of rewards they would genuinely
value.

> Seek feedback and constantly
review the reward structure to
be sure it serves its purpose.

> And remember that a reward is
precisely that – it's not necessarily
what *you* want but *what your
employees will appreciate.*

05

RETAIN

RETAIN

This chapter discusses:

> Retention: how to make it work for the benefit of you and your company

> Motivation and employee engagement

> Appraisals as a tool for motivation and engagement.

Retention, motivation and engagement: it may seem obvious why these three issues are addressed together, or it may seem like an exercise in management or HR speak. On the other hand, some people jump to conclusions about the meaning of these terms and assume that each is something to be desired: this may not necessarily be the case.

The key to retaining staff is understanding what motivates them and using that knowledge to fully engage them with your company and its goals. The challenge, as we've established, is that creative individuals cannot easily be categorised and so you have to somehow take into account individuality while attempting to treat people fairly and consistently within some kind of structure.

When you take a look at your staff, you know instinctively who you'd like to be there in five, ten, fifteen years' time, helping you to run the company. Your instinct will be based on so many different factors – emotional, experiential, anecdotal, practical and others. So it's important to consider how you are going to make this happen.

There are many theories of motivation and as many questionnaires or exercises to assess the motivational drivers of individuals.

As with all things people-related, questionnaires and exercises should always be approached with due caution. You wouldn't or shouldn't use only one method of recruitment selection – for example, it would be unwise to appoint only people who present themselves well and appropriately in a psychometric test. You would be best advised to use a range of methods. Likewise with motivation: you can imagine people fitting into motivational theories like a series of Venn diagrams, and the more tests you have the more complex the overlapping and interaction.

1. RETENTION: HOW TO MAKE IT WORK FOR YOU AND YOUR COMPANY

You could easily be forgiven for assuming that high retention is always something to strive for. I would challenge that view.

RETENTION – A DEFINITION

The ability to retain your staff. High retention means that fewer people leave. It is considered important because the cost of high turnover can be significant in terms of time, productivity and stability.

A certain amount of change is generally good for creative organisations. It acts as a stimulus and a shot of adrenalin. New people provide such an impetus. If you don't have the room for new people then where is that push going to come from?

So, don't just assume that you have to aim for high retention.

BENEFITS OF HIGH RETENTION	DISADVANTAGES OF HIGH RETENTION
Reduced recruitment time and costs	Potentially negative effects on innovation and creativity
Ability to plan staff career development	May be inadvertently discriminatory
Business continuity and succession planning is made easier	Lack of new ideas
Lessens disruption in business planning	Lack of opportunities for staff growth and responsibility
Smoother and more efficient project running	Company may become set in its ways
Development of deeper ongoing relationships with clients and team members	Higher potential for favouritism or nepotism
Enables the development of mutual trust and respect	Tendency to become insular
Deeper social ties	

I am not suggesting that you 'Gotta get rid of the dead wood', as someone once said to me, and that you have to cull 25 per cent of the staff regularly or your creative juices will dry up. But don't be scared of turnover (or 'churn') and use it to your advantage. Hence, the title of this section – making it work for you and your company.

Once again, this will involve a certain amount of thought and planning, so the following checklist should help.

CHECKLIST FOR RETENTION

Who do you have?

> Look at the staff list regularly.

> Put together a simple spreadsheet of roles and skills for all staff members.

> Overlay any career goals and aspirations (see 'appraisals' later in this chapter – an ideal time to gather this information).

Who and what do you need?

> List your immediate needs, but also ponder where the business is going.

> Sort into immediate, short-term, medium-term and long-term needs (these do not have to be detailed or even finite – just an idea or a concept of where the business is going).

> Jot down the kind of skills that you will need in future (these could be task-based skills, or personal attributes, not simply 'must be a whizz at 3D rendering' or 'able to draw out

the talents of more junior staff').

> Think bigger – dare I say it, indulge in some blue sky thinking – from different sectors or different ways of working; this is your chance to plan your creative future and who is going to populate it.

Finally, decide how you are going to fulfil these needs, and access the stream of innovative ideas, creative thought processes, and variety of design solutions to form the unique workplace you may want.

In addition to completing the checklist, it is crucial to gather input from your staff, although perhaps not everyone. (Be careful as to who you choose to include or exclude, and why.) I'm not talking about doing a staff survey. That would not be the most effective way to engage your staff in this process. Sit them down individually in a relaxed environment and get them to talk. Jot down the salient points.

Useful questions to ask

> Why do you work here?

> What is it about this particular company that makes you stay?

> What one thing would make you leave if it changed?

> What do you dislike about the company?

> What would you like to change about the company in the future?

> How would the company look in ten/twenty years' time, if you were in charge?

Think about the most creative person that you know. If they don't work in your company, do you know why they work where they work? Ask them what it is about their place of work that makes them stay.

You may conclude that you are currently perfectly happy with all your team and you want to hang on to them all. That's fine. But it may not always be the case, and the exercise above could make you realise more about your company and your team, and why people want to work with you – or not.

These actions will have provided you with a fair amount of information to take in. Next, you need to do something with it.

2. MOTIVATION AND EMPLOYEE ENGAGEMENT

How can we understand motivation? I could send you in the direction of Abraham Maslow – one of the most frequently quoted exponents of motivational theory, though there are many others. More recent research (e.g. by Herzberg) focuses on the idea of individual motivation, and to me this seems to make sense if you overlay individual experiences in culture, education, upbringing, age and gender.

The main connection between the traditional and current theories is the idea of self-fulfilment. In very simple terms, people will be most motivated by fulfilling their own ideas of success or personal goals of achievement. Obviously, this is intrinsically tied in with the concepts of reward (Chapter 4) and recognition (Chapter 6).

📖 Abraham H Maslow (1943). 'A Theory of Human Motivation', *Psychological Review*.

📖 Frederick Herzberg (1987). 'One More Time: How Do You Motivate Employees?' *Harvard Business Review*, September–October 1987.

MOTIVATION – A DEFINITION

A reason for doing something. That's as simple as it is when it boils down to it. Theories abound, but that will always be the essence.

There are several questionnaires that you can complete or even ask your staff to complete which will pinpoint what drives them. One of the most commonly used is 'Career anchors', devised by Edgar Schein and John Van Maanen. Their system helps people to identify what they are seeking from their job and hence their motivators. The choices are:

> Technical/functional – driven by the need to use and develop particular skills.

> General managerial – driven by the need to get to a level where you can coordinate the efforts of others and identify with the success of the organisation.

> Autonomy/independence – driven by the need to be able to manage or direct your own work; may choose to maintain flexibility rather than take on the added responsibilities promotion may bring.

> Security/stability – driven more by security of job tenure or financial security, than by job content or promotion.

SOURCES OF EMPLOYEE ENGAGEMENT
WHAT MAKES THEM TICK?

> Entrepreneurial creativity – driven by the need to create an organisation or enterprise and use your own abilities to make it a success.

> Service/dedication to a cause – driven by the need to do something that you believe is of value in the world.

> Pure challenge – driven by the need to solve something, by novelty, variety and difficulty, easily bored by easy solutions.

> Lifestyle – driven by the need to achieve balance between personal and work life, making all aspects of your life integrated, may turn down promotion if it endangered that balance.

📖 Edgar H. Schein and John Van Maanen (2013). *Career Anchors: The Changing Nature of Careers Self-Assessment*, John Wiley & Sons.

Employee engagement takes this a step further.

This is all about how you get your staff to do their best work or go 'above and beyond' or the 'extra mile'. You are seeking employees who will voluntarily do more than is strictly expected under their terms of employment. They are likely to do this if they are in some way inspired and have jobs that are of some value.

EMPLOYEE ENGAGEMENT – A DEFINITION

A combination of commitment to the organisation and its values, employee engagement is more than job satisfaction and more than motivation. It is voluntarily offered by the employee, not a part of their terms and conditions of employment.

It is where the employee/employer relationship represents two sides of the same coin: your employee is inspired to greater things and this, in turn, enhances business performance.

It's this win-win aspect of employee engagement which makes it something of a Holy Grail for employers. Who wouldn't want inspired employees, going that extra mile without being hounded to do so? It also includes what's called 'discretionary behaviour'.

DISCRETIONARY BEHAVIOUR – A DEFINITION

This is positive behaviour (usually) on the part of an employee which can be given or withdrawn as the individual wishes and chooses. For example, this could be about the approach to a particular project – the attitude, attention to detail, focus, effort, innovation and whole way of getting the job done.

It's intangible, so hard to measure, and certainly difficult to manage or control.

Engaged employees tend to:

> Help promote your employer brand or reputation – they will be out there in the marketplace singing your praises (we've discussed the

importance of this in relation to recruitment)

> Have a stronger belief in the fairness of the company and a greater trust in their manager – which not only helps build your brand, but also makes it so much easier to get things done

> Focus on their work and produce better results – it's widely agreed that productivity and efficiency is improved by increased employee engagement

> Develop better client relationships – staff who are keen on their work let their enthusiasm shine through, and this is flattering to clients and smooths the way to increased rapport.

In general, being valued and involved appears to be key to a strong sense of engagement. Ideas on how to engage your employees include:

> Follow up on your commitments. If you make a promise, keep it; don't promise what you can't keep. For example, don't promise that someone can go on a particular training course and then change your mind when you realise how much it costs.

> Be fair, consistent and transparent in the way that you deal with staff. This is something of an HR mantra, but a good principle to adopt whenever managing people.

> Make sure that you and others who manage people act in such a way that supports the company and its values. This will help to create an environment or atmosphere that will encourage the kind of behaviour that you are seeking. You are the

example that they will follow. If you show a positive attitude and commitment to the company, this will reinforce its values.

> Give staff the chance to give feedback and have their opinions heard.

> Keep everyone informed about what's going on in the company. This shows trust, particularly if you tell them both the good and the bad. It is simply treating your staff like adults.

> Be conscious of your employees' work/life balance (i.e. ensuring that they are taking holidays, not working long hours regularly) and have some consideration for their health and wellbeing.

> Rather more prosaically, make sure that jobs and tasks are well planned and defined. Everyone has to do boring or repetitive tasks from time to time, but mixing it up as best you can will provide greater interest and meaning. Hence, increased job satisfaction.

As a slight aside, it's important to be realistic: you are likely to come across certain individuals who will never wish to be engaged in their work. This is rare in creative organisations, because of the very nature of the work, but it can still happen. However often you attempt to draw such individuals into your plans for increased engagement, they will dig in their heels and work to rule. It makes much more sense for all concerned that you focus on the people with whom you will have positive results.

Just focus on releasing that positive discretionary behaviour!

CASE STUDY:
Roles to improve engagement

📖 Jane Sparrow (2012).
The Culture Builders, Gower.

In her book The Culture Builders, Jane Sparrow identified five key roles that managers need to adopt in order to increase staff engagement:

> › **The prophet is able to articulate the vision of the future in a way that inspires others.**

> › **The storyteller describes how the vision will be achieved and what it will be like for everyone once it's reached.**

> › **The strategist uses engagement plans for everyone involved to achieve the reality of the vision.**

> › **The coach uses their understanding of individuals to enable and work with them to develop and grow.**

> › **The pilot ensures that the path to the vision is maintained.**

In essence, the identification of these different roles suggests that successful staff engagement requires a number of different approaches to be truly effective – ideally in the form of a plan (which Sparrow discusses in more detail in her book). The focus is on learning as much about your staff as individuals as you can, to help you ensure that there is a strong alignment between their aspirations and the company's vision. Keep listening and talking to them.

The appraisal process, discussed below, can be part of this two-way communication process.

3. APPRAISALS AS A TOOL FOR MOTIVATION AND ENGAGEMENT

A necessary evil; an exercise in time-wasting; a pointless procedure invented by HR; 'we've just got to get through it once a year'. If you approach appraisals with any of these views, it is a fair assumption that it will be a self-fulfilling prophecy!

Why don't **you** like them?
'They take up too much time.'

'They're pointless – I know my team really well and they talk to me about their career goals all the time.'

'Well, we just have to do them, don't we - it's a legal requirement, isn't it?'

'They make me feel really uncomfortable – we're a relaxed office and it doesn't feel right to impose this formal process.'

'It just generates more paperwork – it seems to be just another form filling exercise that we have to do.'

Why don't **they** like them?
'They're pointless – I don't need a formal meeting for someone else to tell me what my career is about.'

'The appraisal meeting always makes me angry – I just get told all the things I did wrong and no one remembers the hard work and contributions I've made.'

'It just focuses on what's gone on recently. We talked about a simple mistake I made two weeks ago, but not about the successful project I led, eight months ago.'

'They only do it for show – the only reason we do it is so we can say we do it. The form just disappears into a file somewhere.'

'There's never any follow-up. We spend time talking about my career and training opportunities, but nothing ever comes of it.'

I've known people who have submitted the same form year after year and their manager has never noticed. In these circumstances, it's no wonder that appraisals are not viewed with pleasure or seen to have any benefits.

Instead of perpetuating these negative views, we need to take a look at performance appraisals and remember their original purpose.

Let's begin by looking at the purpose of appraisals from a broader perspective and gradually narrow it down to understand their real purpose.

Start by thinking about your expectations of your staff. When you hired them, you needed them to fulfil a role (as you took great pains to articulate in the job description). So, you have an idea – ideally, a clear idea – of what you need to see them doing and achieving. If you see them doing well or badly, you are likely to say something to them at the time. This informal day-to-day communication is the first stage of performance management. Perhaps you also jot down these brief informal conversations in a notebook or on your tablet, so you have a full history over the course of time?

In some instances, this may be all that you need to do to keep your staff happy and engaged. However, it is generally recognised that an effective

WHY SHOULD YOU LIKE APPRAISALS?	WHY SHOULD THEY LIKE APPRAISALS?
A chance to really understand the talents and aspirations of your team.	A focus on their career.
A time to enhance the engagement of your team with the company and its goals.	An opportunity to learn and develop.
An opportunity to take part in a positive retention process.	A chance to seek clarity about opportunities and how to achieve goals.
An investment in the future of your company.	An occasion to receive coaching from an expert.
An occasion to learn more about the skills and resources that your company can offer to clients.	A guide on how to succeed in the company.
An opportunity to gain input for your succession plan.	A time to receive positive acknowledgement about good work done.

appraisal system is one of the most successful motivational tools that you have at your disposal as a manager. As a minimum, adopting a process ensures that you treat everyone equally (remember Chapter 2?).

Here is a suggestion of how a performance appraisal might fit into the whole idea of performance management:

1. Ongoing informal day-to-day performance feedback from you to a staff member.

2. Regular or irregular scheduled meetings about work, progress, aspirations, issues, and concerns. These may be weekly or monthly or at any other agreed timeframe.

3. Annual appraisal meeting where objectives are discussed, training needs planned and goals are jointly agreed.

4. Six monthly progress meeting to check in, help remove any barriers, provide additional time or resources, shift deadlines, as fits with the ongoing situation.

5. Then it becomes a circular process – once goals are set, you can regularly check progress, and then set new goals as they are achieved.

DEVELOPING AN APPRAISAL PROCESS

It does not have to be complicated: the most important thing is that it actually works!

The goals are to:

> Have a structured conversation with each staff member to discuss their goals and aspirations

> Make a realistic plan that aligns those goals and aspirations with those of the company

> Highlight any training or development needs that will help to achieve these goals, and

> Put measurements and timeframes into place that will determine progress or achievements.

A form will act as a record and help to form an agenda for the meeting itself, but it can be a simple A4 sheet giving the individual the chance to list their achievements, any issues and where they would like to go next.

Don't get fixated on a form. There are so many examples on various websites that you can end up getting befuddled about what you are trying to achieve. It absolutely does not need to be fourteen pages long, with competency frameworks, assessment criteria and probing questions that seem to have little real point.

Creative people are not big fans of forms, as you will be only too well aware. However, don't forget that one of the purposes of this whole process is to have a record of it to use for future planning.

🅐 Appraisal form

CREATING AN APPRAISAL PROCESS

> **Be clear about what you are appraising**

Does everyone have a job description or similar? What are the standards against which you are appraising people?

It's a fundamental that this information is shared and agreed with each team member. The term 'appraisal' does presuppose that there is some kind of measurement against which the appraisal takes place.

> Decide who is conducting the appraising

Do they know what they are doing? Would they benefit from some training? Individual characters notwithstanding, it's only fair to your staff that the approach by all appraisers is the same.

> Clarify the process

Both appraisers and staff members need to understand the process: what it will entail and what its purpose is. The appraisers may be trained and perhaps involved in the creation of the process, but often the team may have a rather different understanding of its purpose or harbour preconceptions based on past experiences. Some kind of workshop or interactive session with all those involved will help to dispel confusion and, dare I say it, engage people in the process.

Remember: If you ask a question, be sure that there is a reason for it and a purpose for the information that you will obtain. This is particularly the case if you are setting up an appraisal process for the first time.

IMPLEMENTING THE APPRAISAL PROCESS

Remember that the responsibilities are shared across the organisation. You cannot leave all the work to the individual nor can they expect you to take full responsibility for their career. Focus equally on all three main parts of the appraisal process:

> Preparation
> Meeting
> Follow-up.

The main responsibilities and actions for everyone involved in the three steps of the process are described below.

RESPONSIBILITIES OF THE MANAGER/PERSON CONDUCTING THE APPRAISAL

1. Preparation
Seek input about the performance of your team members. Even if you run a small practice, perhaps seek input from team colleagues to be sure you have an accurate and all around view. If this is an annual appraisal, be sure to consider the whole year, not just what happened in the last few months. Seek positive feedback, but don't avoid the negatives. Perhaps prepare some bullet points of the key feedback you need to give.

Read the appraisal form before the meeting – not during it. And don't ignore it altogether, since that clearly does not respect the person who agonised over completing it. Reading it beforehand means that you can consider the contents and make better use of the meeting itself. If there is anything in the form that you react strongly to, you can respond in a more measured way if you've had time to absorb it. You can also

APPRAISALS

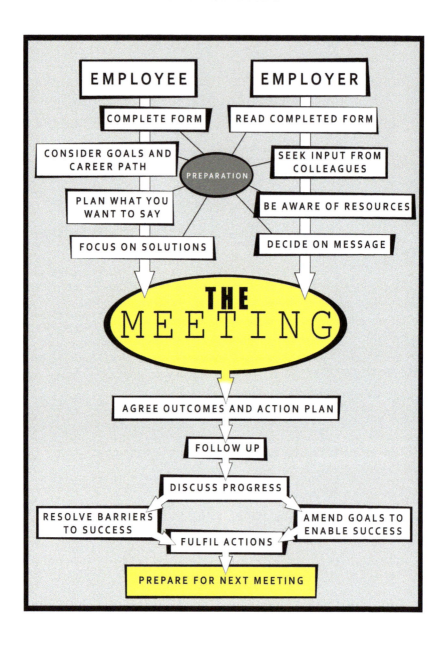

consider solutions or developmental opportunities that might help support the individual's goals.

Make yourself aware of what resources or support may be made available to the individual. There's little point in discussing training courses only to find that there is no money in the budget for them. It may be that there is an internal expert who could help support the person to learn a new skill, or a project they can work on which might expose them to a learning experience.

2. Meeting

Manage the meeting agenda and content. If you've prepared properly, you know what the issues are and can provide feedback, but you may wish to start by asking the staff member how they feel the past year has gone. Let them talk. Offer them feedback. Plan the future.

Manage the meeting timing. Explain the timeframe from the start. If you have scheduled 45 minutes or an hour for the meeting, then stick to it. You can always reconvene.

Listen – this meeting is for the benefit of your staff member. This is their forum to be heard and the focus is on them. Your input is obviously important, but give them the chance to express themselves and give them space.

Ensure that notes are taken. If you have prepared properly, you should have an agenda of points that need to be covered which can serve as the basis for these notes. You can expand on them as the meeting unfolds. It is particularly important that you record giving any feedback, particularly if you

may need to follow up on performance issues. You should also note any goals and the action plan agreed:

> A signed copy of the form and notes ensures that there is no confusion as to what was said and agreed.

Be clear about the outcomes and action plan. Use the concept of SMART goals as a tool. It's important that it's clear who is responsible for doing what and by when. For example, you've agreed that the staff member needs to improve their presentation skills, but how are they going to do so? Are they going to be invited to observe others making presentations to give them insights, and if so who is going to orchestrate that? Are they going on a course, and if so who is going to research relevant courses? In this case, as a manager, you are likely to be more aware of when other presentations may be taking place and have the power to ensure that they are invited; on the other hand, the staff member is perfectly capable of researching different presentation courses and coming back to you with a short list for consideration. Remember this is all about shared responsibility and two-way communication.

SMART goals

Most people may have heard of this term and believe that they understand it or even make use of it. But it is very important that every element of the acronym is included in the goal setting.

continued overleaf ⋯⟶

> SMART was first coined by
George T Doran in 1981. Since
then, the meanings of the letters
have been varied by other
authors, but the original was:

Specific, Measurable, Achievable,
Realistic, Time-related.

🄰 SMART goals worksheet

3. Follow up
Make sure you note down key dates
or deadlines on the action plan. It's
important that you know when these
are so that you can monitor progress.
It is also important to keep to your
side of the bargain and fulfil your own
actions on that plan. If you don't lead by
example, this will perpetuate the myth
that nothing ever happens after the
appraisal meeting itself.

Ensure that the documentation is
properly completed and stored in the
appropriate place – could be with HR
or in some other confidential location –
with the other personnel records.

Make a note in your diary to check in
with the team member after a couple
of weeks or a month to be sure that
they know you are taking these actions
seriously. When you follow this through,
it will prompt them to pursue their own
part of the bargain.

RESPONSIBILITIES OF THE EMPLOYEE – WHAT YOU SHOULD EXPECT FROM THEM

1. Preparation
> Attend the workshop explaining
the process or at least read the
supporting notes.

> Complete the form fully and with
proper thought about what is
realistic. (This is not supposed
to be an opportunity to raise all
the negative issues that the staff
member may have.)

> Give some thought to goals and how
these might be achieved. Again, a
touch of reality helps here.

2. Meeting
> Be prepared to discuss
achievements, barriers, and goals.
The meeting won't work if they are
not prepared to talk.

> Take responsibility for their
own career and how to achieve
aspirations. (Ultimately, it is their
career and you are merely an
enabler.)

> Welcome feedback and constructive
criticism as an opportunity to learn.

3. Follow up
> Fulfil the agreed action points within
the agreed timeframe. If there
is some barrier to doing so, they
should come back to you to explain
and discuss how it can be overcome.

> Show a positive attitude towards
making the appraisal process work.
Indifference or cynicism are the
opponents here.

> Genuinely engage in developmental
goals and responding to the
feedback given by trying to change
behaviour and performance levels
to suit.

WHAT'S NEXT?

Above all, keep the communication
going. The rapport you have with your

team should increase. By no means treat this as an exercise in being everyone's best friend. The intention is to focus on career goals within the parameters of what is feasible within your company. Don't promise the moon, because you can't deliver it.

Bywords such as honesty and transparency are invaluable in ensuring that an atmosphere of trust is developed and maintained with your team.

Ideally, you can take a look at the outcomes of the appraisals in terms of goals, and you'll notice that there are some common themes across a team or all staff. It may be that there is a perceived need for a particular type of training – a particular software, perhaps, or some kind of management training.

There will be other more esoteric aspirations which may be better realised if a mentor is appointed. Soft skills can also be addressed with coaching to a certain extent.

You'll be able to maintain some faith in the appraisal process if you aim for some quick wins:

> A role might come up on a project that someone expressed an interest in fulfilling; perhaps they could do so with some guidance from a more senior team member, or join a team that can initiate them in the skills required.

> Ask your resident software expert to schedule time with someone who wants to learn more, and make sure that the project resourcing enables this.

> Organise a lunchtime session and talk about your own experiences on a particular project type.

> Consider whether you can act as a mentor in leadership or management skills.

There is an awful lot written about 'learning organisations' (a term coined by Peter M Senge and his colleagues), but like most trends the underlying principle is really very simple: try to keep up the momentum and communication about development and learning!

> Create a working environment in which learning and development is encouraged, valued and second nature.

> Every company can be a learning organisation. You can organise shared trips to exhibitions or lectures without too much effort or too much cost. You can ask those who have been on courses to give a talk about what they've learned. You can lend books, magazines and DVDs on creative topics. There are also many free webinars online on various topics.

> Encourage and support learning and development.

> Recognise those who have really made an effort to enhance their skills and knowledge.

🔲 Peter M Senge (1990), *The Fifth Discipline: The art and practice of the learning organization*, Doubleday.

SUMMARY: PLAN TO RETAIN

Retention, motivation and employee engagement are intrinsically linked and a well-designed appraisal process will positively support your efforts to retain those employees you wish to retain, motivate them and engage them in their work, and engender demonstrative positive discretionary behaviour.

Rather than approaching appraisals as if they were a chore, plan them well and use all their positive aspects to the benefit of your company. These are people businesses we are talking about, so if you run a business you need to know and properly engage with your people.

Remember these three factors, which work in your favour as well as your employees':

> Do your planning

> Re-do your planning

> Continue to think short term but don't ignore medium to long term.

Encourage your team members to expand their horizons and enhance their knowledge on a whole range of subjects. This will create increased dynamism in your working environment. It will not only engage, but energise, your staff. Happy, motivated employees will maximise their discretionary behaviour and enhance the service you can provide to your clients.

06

RECOGNISE

RECOGNISE

This chapter discusses:

> What to recognise and how to do it
> Leadership and promotion
> Succession planning.

RECOGNITION – A DEFINITION

A reinforcement of the contribution that a member of staff has made towards your company in terms of behaviour or services. By positively acknowledging this behaviour or service, you are hoping that it will be repeated or perpetuated. Recognition differs from reward in that it can often be non-tangible, such as public thanks or congratulations.

Recognition often sits with reward in HR publications, but in this book I've chosen to make a distinction between employee *reward* as a tangible expression, and employee *recognition* in terms of acknowledging when someone's actions and behaviour have had a positive impact on the organisation.

Recognition can stretch from being named and thanked at a staff meeting or via a company-wide email which can be used for all staff, to promotion to partner or other level of management, which is clearly going to be limited to a smaller number of staff.

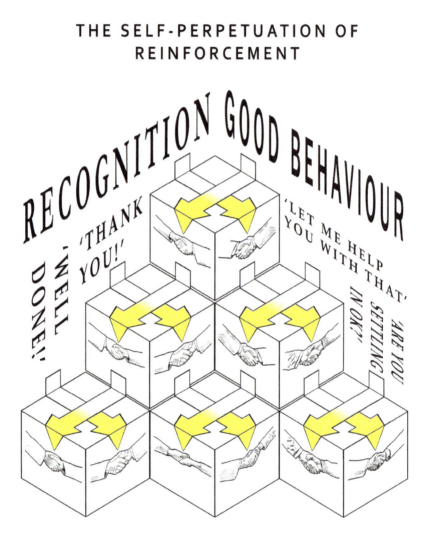

1. WHAT TO RECOGNISE AND HOW TO DO IT

Let's take a look at what you might want to recognise. Remember the appraisal process that we discussed in Chapter 5? What did you identify as the key criteria by which to judge someone's performance? There are likely to be some similar elements here, but recognition is about effort as well as achievement. So, the person who mopped up in the office after the boiler leaked on a weekend may be recognised as well as the person who worked through the night to make sure that a last minute new business proposal was submitted on time.

The table below presents some ideas about actions or behaviour you might want to recognise. These are merely examples and you can easily spend some time thinking of reasons to recognise someone that will be specific and pertinent to your own company. Remember, it's about acknowledging behaviour and activities that you want to perpetuate. The power of positive reinforcement.

INTERNAL BEHAVIOURS	EXTERNAL BEHAVIOURS
Company community: Brings cakes or flowers into work to share; prompts everyone to remember birthdays and anniversaries; organises regular social events.	Professional legacy: Lectures at the local university or acts as mentor to graduates; supports continuous professional development (CPD) or coaches for professional exams.
Collegiate attitude: Provides professional and/or emotional support to team members; positively supports the company's culture and attitude.	Community outreach: Develops relationships with local charities that support your company's ethos; represents the company in leading or working on projects for the local community.
Coaching/sharing knowledge: Volunteers to coach peers in areas of expertise; shares own knowledge and experience to the benefit of the team.	Business community: Is an active member of a professional organisation; represents the company at networking events; delivers lectures and talks at industry related events.
Action outside their role: Regularly making colleagues cups of tea; cleaning the fridge; joining a team temporarily and taking on whatever tasks they were given in order to help meet deadlines; senior person fulfilling junior role to be sure project deadlines are achieved; designer volunteering to answer the phone when the receptionist is off sick.	

ACKNOWLEDGEMENT

Having decided on behaviours that are worthy of recognition, it is important to give some thought to how you might approach recognition as acknowledgement.

PRIVATE THANKS

This is generally in the form of communication:

> Face to face/one to one

> Telephone call

> Email

> Written note/card.

You are favourably acknowledging a particular action or behaviour. In these email-driven days, it is generally accepted that a handwritten note or card from someone – especially from a busy manager or leader – will be considered of higher value than an email or even a face to face conversation. It provides a written record that can be read and kept. Although this should be positively received by most people, there are always exceptions who may take umbrage for some reason. Another consideration is that, although it is acknowledgement of a sort, a note is probably the least effective method precisely because it is private.

PUBLIC THANKS

This is acknowledgement of an individual in a public forum of their peers, such as:

> Staff/studio meeting

> Project team meeting

> Team/staff email

> Company intranet

> Company newsletter

> Company noticeboard.

As a form of recognition, it is generally deemed to be more effective because it is carried out in public. You are indicating and positively reinforcing behaviour or actions that you value and thereby hoping that these will be perpetuated and copied by other people.

However, a word of warning: if you are acknowledging someone's role on a project or in another team initiative, be sure that you are thanking the right person.

PEER RECOGNITION

As the name suggests, this would be proposed by fellow staff members. I'm not suggesting 'Employee of the Month', but something a bit more creative. It could be monthly, or quarterly or over whatever time period you wish. It could be for the person who's been the best mentor to their team, someone who's just gone out of their way to help other people, someone who's always positive, or one of those people who is a pleasure to work with. Let your team decide. Peer recognition can often be more meaningful than company or managerial recognition, and as effective.

CASE STUDY:
Recognising the team

Three architectural technicians realise that the graduate recruits are struggling with their company's bespoke software. They each offer to spend their spare time - lunch hours, early morning or after work - with one of the three new recruits. After a month or so, and a significant improvement in the graduates' level of comfort with the software and their rate of work, one of the technicians sends an email to his team leader to tell her about the scheme.

She mentions it in a resourcing meeting in front of the MD. At the next staff meeting, the MD speaks at some length about the selfless efforts of the one technician who had sent the email.

Simply because he had not done his homework and looked into the situation further, he created significant resentment in two staff members, and embarrassment in one. This was not a successful exercise in recognition.

DEVELOPING A RECOGNITION CULTURE

Recognition should be available for everyone, but is ideally about individuals. This is also why you should not include staff social events or outings in a recognition programme. You are distinguishing between individuals whose contributions have gone above and beyond, and those who are simply doing their job.

As always, don't discriminate (see Chapter 2).

Here are some tips to help you with your programme of recognition:

> Include all members of staff. It is remarkably common to ignore support staff in these initiatives. Consider the divisive message that this delivers and how that will affect retention among the support staff. All levels and types of staff are capable of reinforcing the standards of behaviour and activity that you are seeking to embed in your company.

> Be sure of the standards that you are recognising and seeking to reinforce. Relate the action or behaviour to its business impact and why it reinforces your company's standards of values and ethics.

> Be consistent in recognising the behaviour or action that you've said you will. This is why doing your research is very important: elicit input from your fellow leaders to be sure you're not missing the person who's hiding their light under a bushel.

> Try to be prompt and timely with recognition so it is clear what is being reinforced and acknowledged.

> Ideally, try not to make this solely manager-driven. If there is input

from staff too, this will make it less likely to come across as favouritism or simply the next person on the rota for recognition (which is why 'Employee of the Month' will rarely work in creative organisations).

> Don't recognise someone for the wrong reasons. If they've worked through the night as a one-off to meet a shifting deadline or similar, then that is fair enough, but if they worked through the night because they were mucking around all day, then that's a different matter!

PITFALLS TO AVOID – RECOGNITION

> **Mysteriously giving recognition to an employee for no apparent reason. The reason may be obvious to you, but is it clear to other members of staff? Be clear about the basis for your choice.**

> **Repeatedly recognising the same person or group of people and ignoring others.**

> **Recognising only those who trumpet their contributions via company-wide emails or other wide-ranging methods.**

> **Provoking canvassing for recognition by certain staff members.**

> **Diluting the recognition by spreading it too wide. Saying 'Great job, great job, you're all great' may work as a transitory feel-good tactic, but people soon disregard meaningless words.**

> **Sapping enthusiasm by making the reason or criteria confusing or non-existent.**

A WORD ABOUT TIME OFF

Time off is an intangible benefit, so this is the best place to discuss it.

Time off in lieu or, indeed, additional time off is sometimes used by companies as a form of recognition for a job well done, particularly if it involved working long hours towards a deadline or similar time-related contributions.

There is nothing wrong with this, providing the right person or people are considered.

However, try not to engender an environment where expecting and even accumulating 'time in lieu' becomes a habit. I've known situations where individuals have been given time off on one occasion and subsequently requested an additional week's time off because they had worked additional hours in order to 'save up' this time. Be clear that one instance does not create a new policy.

2. LEADERSHIP AND PROMOTION

THE NATURE OF LEADERSHIP

We tend to assume that everyone would view promotion and involvement in leadership to be a plus and something to aspire to. This may not necessarily be the case. There are those who are perfectly happy to keep out of the limelight and would prefer not to have the additional responsibility that promotion brings.

Conversely, there are people whose desire for promotion takes them on a furious path of one-upmanship. More often than not this is to the detriment of positive working relationships with their peers and sometimes with questionable ethics. They may also completely miss the point about the additional responsibility that promotion brings.

I suppose it's possible that an unwilling leader will be successful, but it's not a good start. I'd also suggest that you should not bow to the pressure of those desperately seeking promotion; their 'enthusiasm' is not a good enough reason in itself to promote them. Do you really want to be held over a barrel by someone who approaches you with 'if you don't promote me, I'm leaving'?

It can be a difficult call. Many books advise people that they need to pursue a path of self-promotion to ensure that their positive characteristics and strengths are known to the decision-makers. However, this implies limitations on the abilities of the decision-makers to conduct their own research and make their own observations. If you work in an environment where regularly sticking your head above the parapet seems to be the only way to get ahead and is seen as 'pro-active', then humility and self-effacing behaviour is clearly not going to help you get ahead. But it does also suggest laziness on the part of those who are looking to promote the next generation of leaders.

As a manager, you should be making it a priority to get to know your staff, and their strengths and weaknesses. Just because someone is quiet, doesn't mean they wouldn't make a good manager or leader.

There is also a school of thought that 'Leaders are born, not made'. Much has been written to support both sides of that argument.

Instead of focusing on trends and theories, it is important to be clear about what a 'Leader' looks like in your company. It cannot be stressed enough that the way existing leadership behaves serves as an example of success to those who aspire to greatness. If you shout at members of staff in public, express anger in the studio, put people down, are moody, uncommunicative, needy, lazy or indulge in any of a whole host of negative behaviours, there is every chance that this will be seen as acceptable and a possible route to leadership. This is an additional burden on leaders – that they are under the microscope. Not only is the weight of the business and its failure or success on your shoulders, but how you cope with that leadership is always under scrutiny.

THE STRUCTURE OF LEADERSHIP

I mentioned in Chapter 3 that it is best to avoid allotting titles for the sake of it, because it can create an unnecessarily hierarchical organisation structure with lots of tiers that are rather unnecessary. The days of architecture practices being structured as a series of lengthy apprenticeships are largely gone. Promotion and recognition are no longer dinosaur awards. Certainly, in creative companies, we tend to prefer to work in much flatter organisations where communication and interaction is simpler and more direct. In this way, creativity is enhanced by collaboration.

However, you do need to give this some thought. If you create lots of tiers of management, you may end up with a situation where everyone has a title and it becomes rather meaningless. Look at the size of your organisation. If it's relatively small, you have no need to have more than one or two levels. There is no magic formula; just consider the hierarchy that you are creating.

If you want a truly interactive, collaborative workplace, too many levels will hinder that creative spirit.

So, what do titles mean? You have junior, intermediate and senior; you have associate, senior associate and partner; you have architect, senior architect, project architect, associate director, director and partner. It's never ending and has infinite permutations.

If promotion is to be of value and seen as some kind of genuine recognition, then it has to have some kind of purpose.

THE VALUE OF A TITLE

We're all aware of those companies where everyone seems to be a director or a vice president. I once knew someone who would have almost sold their soul to the devil in order to have the title of director. Eventually, the person was made a director … and so were five other people in this twenty-person company. What worth does that put on such a title?

On the other hand, a title costs nothing – and titles mean a lot to some people. You do need to consider the effects of succumbing to the constant bleating of a member of staff that they should be a manager or associate or whatever, thinking that 'it's only a title'. You still need to compare like with like.

The most rational approach when thinking about titles or promotion is to remember that people will judge the situation according to their peers. They may not be particularly bothered about having a title until they see someone who they believe to be their equal obtaining a title. And, if it is not clear why that title exists, then you are just creating a rod for your own back. I suppose there is something charmingly egalitarian about everyone having a title, but it does seem a bit unnecessary.

WHAT ARE YOU TRYING TO ACHIEVE? WHY PROMOTE SOMEONE AT ALL?

As with recognition, promotion works by trying to positively reinforce behaviour or actions that you want to see replicated. In this instance, you are very publicly and permanently recognising someone because you believe that they have a long-term contribution to make to your company and also because you believe that they have demonstrated the ability to assume managerial responsibilities. Promotion indicates abilities beyond simply doing a good job. This is not just about being the best salesperson or the best designer.

THE PETER PRINCIPLE

No, this is not a principle that Peter is the most common name held by leaders. In 1968, Dr Laurence J Peter, a Canadian professor, co-authored with Raymond Hull, a humorous book entitled *The Peter Principle: Why Things Always Go Wrong*. His basic premise was that, in an organisation's hierarchy, employees will rise or be promoted to the level of their incompetence.

That is, people keep getting promoted as they remain competent, but eventually they will be promoted to a job that is too challenging for them or beyond their capabilities. Employees rise to their own level of incompetence and stay there. As Peter puts it:

'In a hierarchy, every employee tends to rise to his level of incompetence ... in time every post tends to be occupied by an employee who is incompetent to carry out its duties ... Work is accomplished by those employees who have not yet reached their level of incompetence.'

This is not necessarily about incompetence as such; rather it demonstrates that different positions in the hierarchy require different skills which some may not possess. Hence, it is important to consider the requirements for proposed roles rather than simply promoting on the basis of success in the existing role.

Laurence J Peter and Raymond Hull (1969). *The Peter Principle: Why Things Always Go Wrong*, William Morrow & Co.

Responsibility and management are key words. You need to consider whether individuals are capable of and willing to assume responsibility, and whether they have or can quickly develop management skills.

Take some time to note down what you would be looking for if you promoted someone. This is what you would be recognising if you chose to do so. Remember that they will be epitomising the values of your company. And also, be sure that the criteria you use for promotion are not discriminatory.

Although the criteria that you chose for the appraisal system may offer you some guidelines, this is a different process.

THE IMPORTANCE OF THE PERSON

One major way in which it is different, is that you need to be much more conscious of personal attributes or characteristics. This can be about the person and not just their performance.

Let me give you some examples of characteristics you might be looking for:

> **Dependability/reliability**: They don't fly off the handle at the slightest thing or cause people around them to feel they have to tread on eggshells because of the volatility of their moods.

> **Respect for others**: They don't dismiss other people's viewpoints out of hand, they listen to their

team. This does not preclude passion for a particular topic or opinion.

> **Decision-making**: Avoiding making timely decisions or addressing problems may often make the outcome worse. Again, there is a difference between considered and informed decision-making and diving in without due consideration.

> **Integrity**: Aside from the expectation that someone in a leadership role within your company would behave in an ethically and morally appropriate way, you also don't want them to abuse their position or throw their weight around expecting privileges and attention.

> **Flexibility**: Not being swayed by the opinion of the last person that they spoke to, but able to take into account the opinions of others, able to deal with changes in circumstances, roll with the punches and cope with the ups and downs that current business practice may involve.

> **Charisma/gravitas**: It is rightly said that you can't be a leader without any followers. You may not have a Nelson Mandela or Martin Luther King in your company, but does the person command any respect? Do people listen when they speak? Are their opinions valued? Is their expertise valued?

> **Consideration towards others**: This could be acting as a coach or mentor; it could be noticing when a team member is upset and needs to talk about something. It is also about encouraging new members of staff and facilitating their entry to the company.

You simply need to decide what the priorities are for your company.

PROMOTION CRITERIA

Often when it comes to promotion there is a lot of agonising over what a particular criterion means or what the difference is between levels – what does a director do as opposed to an associate director or a senior associate as opposed to an associate? What does it mean to be a partner? This is likely to vary between companies, but certain expectations of responsibility and behaviour are pretty universal.

Promotion criteria can change over time as the business evolves. Like so many people-related things, if you give it your best shot and communicate it well, you will have a good chance of it working for you.

Typical criteria include:

> **Significant contribution in an area of the business**: For example design, management, technical, new business development. This is likely to be the main focus of the individual's job.

> **Bringing in business**: Some companies will put an extra weighting on this criterion if it is an intrinsic expectation of the company's management that they bring in work.

> **Coaching/mentoring**: This criterion will measure the level to which the individual helps to develop talent and fosters the future of the company. They should demonstrate a willingness to share information and experience so that those who have more to learn can do so.

> **Interpersonal skills**: 'Plays well with others' as mentioned in Chapter 4. It really should be a prerequisite for any person holding a senior role within an organisation to have strong interpersonal skills and show a high level of what is now called 'emotional intelligence'.

> **Contribution to the company**: What do they do in addition to their day-to-day job? This is where you really need to steer clear of recognising someone simply because they are always working late or attending out-of-hours training or travelling regularly for the company. Some staff members – often women – may not be able to do this because of personal responsibilities. You may run into trouble if they are carers or have parental responsibilities. Remember that it is possible to do an excellent job within working hours and still make an increased contribution in other ways, such as creativity and innovation.

These criteria should be clear. Ideally, they should be clearly communicated too, so that everyone is aware of what to aspire to and what is being recognised when someone is promoted.

PRACTICAL ADVICE:
Promotion criteria for an associate

> Demonstrates expertise in a particular role

> Supports CPD and willingly shares own expertise and knowledge

> Communicates actively, effectively and responsively and encourages two-way communication

> Leads the appraisal process for team and fully supports and enables team development

> Delegates, offering appropriate levels of support, authority and autonomy

> Develops strong and durable client relationships

> Shows innovation and creativity in client solutions in response to client needs

> Shows strong awareness of client perspective

> Demonstrates, expects and supports high quality of work and best practice

> Actively pursues new business opportunities and/or ongoing or additional work for existing clients

> Positive contribution towards the preparation of proposals and pitches for work.

Obviously, every company will have its own priorities, but it is common to expect that as the level of responsibility in the company grows there will be an increase in business understanding and usually increased involvement in the marketing and new business aspects of running the business. Not everyone is good or successful at networking, but all leaders should be able to at least help write proposals using their knowledge of the company's work and understanding of what a particular client would value.

THE BENEFITS OF USING CRITERIA

You don't need to use specific criteria and have no obligation to write it all down and stick to it. It may seem much easier simply to promote those people that you know will be good for the company in the future. But here are some risks if you don't use clearly articulated criteria:

> **Discrimination**: It may be inadvertent, but is more likely to occur without the use of objective criteria.

> **Reputation**: Your company reputation will be affected one way or another by who you choose to promote, since they represent you. The wrong choice will reflect badly on you.

> **Nepotism/favouritism**: Promoting only the people in your family or social group limits your field of choice and may not be the best selection for the job.

> **Likely to be ineffective**: Regardless of how good your gut instinct is, you may miss vital flaws in the individual's skills or

characteristics which may lead to the appointment failing.

> **Costly exercise**: The cost of getting it wrong in terms of time and therefore money, not to mention potential claims of discrimination and damage to your reputation, could be huge.

Another way of looking at it, is to look out for some danger signs or things to avoid.

WARNING SIGNS – PROMOTION

> **People are evasive when asked about this person.**

> **The person is trying too hard to be liked (viz. David Brent in** *The Office***).**

> **Poor people skills – even the most talented genius still has to work with other people in most companies. You need to decide if you can deal with the fallout of rudeness and general bad behaviour. It may depend on the extent of the behaviour and whether this person can be kept isolated to prevent or reduce clashes with those around them.**

> **People avoid working with them or simply avoid them – no one can work in isolation, least of all someone who is supposed to be managing people.**

> **They are the subject of ridicule and office banter. This doesn't lend itself to being taken seriously as a manager.**

> **They indulge in gossip about the company and its leaders.**

A definite no no: they should be leading by example.

> They are argumentative and do not support leadership decisions in public. I'm not suggesting you should only promote 'yes men', but there is a difference between a healthy debate in an appropriate meeting or private space, and the management team presenting a disunited front.

> They are always complaining – managing a company has challenges enough without having a victim attitude to deal with too.

> They are unable to take constructive criticism. Someone who has a heightened view of their own value will expect more than they give in return.

> They don't keep promises. This kind of behaviour will badly damage any attempts you make at employee engagement.

> They don't have any gravitas at all. Gravitas is the ultimate intangible, but we've all met managers or directors who have the charisma of a wet sponge and they do not reflect well on their company's choice.

Ultimately, ask yourself what this person is going to add to the leadership of your company.

3. SUCCESSION PLANNING

Succession planning became a buzz phrase in management speak several years ago, but it remains something of a mystery and many companies still ignore the issue until late in the day. It's also been said that many truly creative individuals will never want to retire because they love what they do so much, so what's the point in focusing on their successors. It's almost an admission of their own mortality!

SUCCESSION PLANNING – A DEFINITION

> The CIPD definition is:

'A process for identifying and developing potential future leaders or senior managers, as well as individuals to fill other business-critical positions, either in the short- or the long-term.'

> It is about looking to the future of the company and protecting business continuity.

Of course, not every leader or leadership team will want to perpetuate their company. Some may see the future of their company simply as a pension plan. But there will be others who see that they have a responsibility to their staff to consider the future and also who may wish to try to have some control over their legacy.

SUCCESSION PLANNING

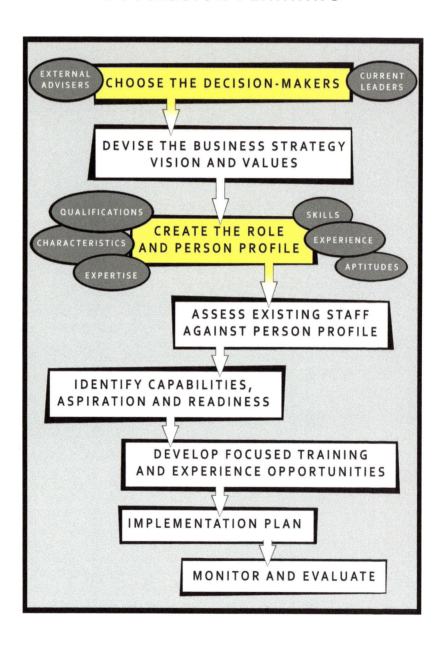

EXTERNAL ADVISERS

CHOOSE THE DECISION-MAKERS

CURRENT LEADERS

DEVISE THE BUSINESS STRATEGY VISION AND VALUES

QUALIFICATIONS

CHARACTERISTICS

EXPERTISE

CREATE THE ROLE AND PERSON PROFILE

SKILLS

EXPERIENCE

APTITUDES

ASSESS EXISTING STAFF AGAINST PERSON PROFILE

IDENTIFY CAPABILITIES, ASPIRATION AND READINESS

DEVELOP FOCUSED TRAINING AND EXPERIENCE OPPORTUNITIES

IMPLEMENTATION PLAN

MONITOR AND EVALUATE

Easy steps to successful succession planning:

1. Don't ignore it.
2. Decide how much influence you are going to have on the plan.
3. Decide who is going to determine the future. Should it be internal input only or would some external guidance offer additional value?
4. Decide whether your current staff should have input. Often more junior staff have no input into the future of a company with which they could potentially have a long and successful career. This is almost the inverse of succession planning.
5. Taking into account likely changes in the economy and the industry, agree some basic idea of what kind of company is needed to face the future.
6. Agree what company culture is to be perpetuated or developed for the future. This is where you have to make some big decisions. It's about deciding what to keep and what to discard with regard to the company as it's got this far.
7. Discuss and have a clear idea of what skills are needed to run a company. This will be a mixture of task-related and people-related skills, both hard and soft skills.
8. Discuss and try to articulate the type of character or person profile that will be needed to lead the company. At this stage, you can be idealistic – although, trying to balance that with a touch of reality does make things rather easier.

Once you've gone through the planning exercise, you can begin to implement the plan.

FREQUENTLY ASKED QUESTIONS ABOUT SUCCESSION PLANNING

Q. What sort of timeframe is best? How soon before I retire should I start planning?
A. There is no definitive answer to this. You must temper the need to give adequate time to prepare a successor with the level of their ambition to get started. You need time to be sure that they are ready by having sufficient experience and training, but also you don't want them champing at the bit to get rid of you before you are ready to leave. It will probably depend on the level of additional experience and training that the individual needs.

Q. What is the rate of success of those companies who've actually tried to put a plan into place?
A. This is mixed. Companies that are working through their third or fourth generation are still learning from their previous experiences. Some get it right first time. The plan needs to be solid but also flexible enough to cope with change – for example, if your favoured candidate decides to leave the company.

Q. Isn't succession planning only for large companies?
A. More formal succession plans may be needed in larger companies, but even in smaller companies some level of planning is a better assurance of the future of the business than simply leaving it to fate and circumstance. It may seem obvious to you that the next most senior person is going to inherit your role, but there will remain issues

of timing, handover and what path the company is going to take.

Q. Should I tell everyone that there is a succession plan?

A. This can go both ways. Those who are not included may demonstrate their disgruntlement and even leave, unless the reasons why they are not involved are explained sensitively and are genuinely transparent; those who are involved may develop expectations that ultimately they are unable to fulfil. However, you do need to tell people who you have identified that you have done so. A thorough and objective planning process, good communication, and transparency are your friends here.

Q. Should I tell the people I've identified as my successors that they are?

A. Yes. See above. They may not wish to be told but, on balance, it is usually better to over communicate than under communicate. The rest of the office need not be made aware if the potential successor so wishes.

Q. What kind of transition period should there be?

A. Once you've identified the individual/s and you feel that they are ready to assume increased responsibility, you can plan it with them. Opinions vary as to whether a transition period should take place whereby you hand over nominal responsibility to the individual while you are still around to support and guide, or if you simply stand by your judgement and hand over the reins completely.

Q. Can I still maintain an involvement in the practice or company once I'm no longer in charge?

A. This is obviously related to the question above. Assume that you've handed over responsibility completely and someone else is in charge. You do need to think carefully about how often you dabble in the company, if at all. You should at least give the new leader a chance to establish themselves as the new person in charge. If you are still regularly popping into the office, it will make the transition all the more difficult because people may still defer to you with any problems or decision-making, or even try to play you off against the new incumbent.

SUCCESSION MAY BE A TEAM EFFORT

The future of the company may not need to be in the hands of one person. Successful succession plans could result in at least two individuals taking charge.

A common division of responsibility is internal versus external: one person tasked with running the company, keeping a tight rein on finances, quality, internal processes, and so on; and the other focusing on maintaining the profile of the company, developing a strong network of professional connections and most of all providing a stream of work. This means that each person can use their strengths.

However you choose to do it, the leadership will need support from individuals whose skills and abilities will fill any gaps or weaknesses. This is a team effort.

A word of warning: it does help if one person is ultimately in charge. Of the two or three or however many chosen as successors, there does need to be an individual who has final responsibility and decision-making power. Otherwise, you may never move forward with any plans.

Succession planning need not be a complex issue. It could be as simple as the senior partner or business owner identifying their own successor. This may work well and be all that is needed. However, this has been known to fail as we've seen with some high-profile organisations.

CASE STUDY:
Unintended consequences

The long-serving managing director of a large architecture practice is nearing retirement. He is unsure which of his senior management team will be best at taking the company forward. He decides that a team of four will be put in charge for a period of a year and given the chance to prove themselves. After a year, one will be appointed managing director to succeed him.

He is effectively setting them up against each other. Over the year, the staff are subjected to a series of divergent initiatives, profile-grabbing activities, empire building, political posturing and generally divisive behaviour. The company's reputation and profits slide. Once the year has passed, a choice is made. A choice that almost inevitably 75 per cent of the staff disagree with; and they vote with their feet. The company does ultimately survive, but at some cost in finances, reputation and emotional turmoil for all concerned.

The lesson to be learned: don't be lazy and hedge your bets. If you are going to appoint a successor, do so. They don't have to be perfect. Their team can provide additional skills and expertise.

How you approach recognition, promotion and succession planning can have far reaching effects on your company's employer brand. Use the opportunities that you have to plan these aspects of your business wisely.

> What and who you recognise mirrors the values of your company.

> A structured recognition programme protects you from pitfalls such as discrimination or damage to your reputation.

> Never forget the value of a simple 'Thank you'.

> Always include all the staff in your recognition programme.

> Effort as well as achievement can be valued.

> In terms of promotion, make it the exception rather than the norm. Titles should be special and deserved. They should be open to everyone to strive for, but with clear objective criteria for achievement.

> Never forget the importance of research and planning.

> Communication should be regular, considered and clear on all the topics discussed in this chapter.

07

RELEASE / RETURN

RELEASE/RETURN

Throughout this book, I've really tried to focus on the positive aspects of HR and people management. This is partly to dispel the myth that HR is only about negative or unpleasant activities, but also to show the genuine force for good that HR can be for your business. However, there comes a time when what might be perceived to be more negative issues have to be faced head on.

And that is an important point to make. If there are problems of some sort with individuals or the business, there is rarely a positive outcome from ignoring them and hoping they'll go away of their own accord. Of course, there are always exceptions, but typically problems fester and just get worse.

I'm sure you've experienced the able but largely anti-social intermediate designer who is hard to staff on projects because people just don't want to work with them. Often, because the problem is not specifically related to performance, and is quite personal and difficult to articulate, it will be ignored and the person may be passed around from project to project until there's nowhere else for them to go. That's when the frustration with the situation boils over and HR gets a call saying 'they just have to go!'. If HR had been involved sooner and the problem raised earlier, there may have been a less drastic solution.

So, the topics addressed in this chapter are:

> Addressing problems and performance management, including sickness absence management
> Disciplinary and grievance issues
> Release: in terms of dismissal, redundancy and resignation
> Return.

Before I go any further, I should mention that the title of this chapter is a misnomer, because release may not be the ultimate conclusion of some of the procedures we're going to talk about; but it might be and that's something that those involved need to be aware of from early on. But let's not focus on this as an unstoppable train, there are always stages along the way at which processes can be stopped and directions changed.

1. ADDRESSING PROBLEMS AND PERFORMANCE MANAGEMENT

It would be vain to think that I could list all the problems that you might ever have and offer solutions for them. Rather, the intention here is to give examples of some of the most common problems, and also to put tools at your disposal that you can use as might seem appropriate in the particular circumstance.

COMMON PROBLEMS THAT APPEAR DIFFICULT TO ADDRESS

LONG-TERM OR REGULAR SICKNESS ABSENCE

There seems to be a fear that you cannot address sickness as an issue.

You can. However, it can be relatively complex depending on the specific circumstances. Simple guidance would be:

> Be conscious of your responsibilities under the Equality Act and potential disability discrimination.
> Be sure to seek input from the staff member.
> Seek professional input – ask for a GP report or fund an occupational health (OH) assessment. You cannot rely on your own research or the staff member's interpretation of what their GP has said.
> Consider reasonable adjustments or temporary changes to the employee's role, tasks or methods of working, even if their condition is not a formal disability.
> If in any doubt, seek the advice of an employment lawyer.

Ultimately, if someone is unable to carry out their job because of illness, it is not impossible to dismiss them from employment, but you must be sure to consider all other options first.

REASONABLE ADJUSTMENTS: WHAT ARE THEY?

Reasonable adjustments will differ from case to case and you should discuss them with your employee using their input and the information from the GP report or OH assessment.

Examples might include:

> Doing things another way – e.g.

allowing someone with social anxiety disorder to have their own desk instead of hot-desking

> Redesigning the job role – e.g. so that there is no lifting involved for someone who has developed chronic back problems

> Considering flexible working options – e.g. enabling a person with multiple sclerosis to change their hours of work so that they don't have to travel and be jostled in the rush hour

> Making physical changes – e.g. installing a ramp for a wheelchair user or an audio-visual fire alarm for a deaf person

> Letting a disabled person work somewhere else – e.g. on the ground floor for a wheelchair user

> Changing their equipment – e.g. providing a special keyboard for an arthritis sufferer

> Allowing employees who become disabled to make a phased return to work – e.g. working flexible hours or part-time

> Offering employees training opportunities, recreation and refreshment facilities.

POOR ATTITUDE

This can be difficult to address because it is tricky to articulate or pin down. The secret is to stick to the business impact and the impression or perception of the person's behaviour or actions. For example, saying: 'When you are being briefed on your role on this project, you do not seem to be giving your full attention and so seem uninterested. This gives a very negative impression to the person briefing you and the rest of the team.'

CONFLICT BETWEEN TWO INDIVIDUALS

It may seem like a good idea to get them both in the same room to 'thrash it out', and it might work, but there is a greater chance that it will just exacerbate the situation, or there will only be a superficial fix reached. Try a more subtle approach such as mediation if you want a long-lasting outcome. Don't expect people to become bosom buddies, your goal is that they work well together, anything else is a bonus.

HOW PERFORMANCE MANAGEMENT HELPS TO SOLVE PROBLEMS

In Chapter 5 we discussed the ongoing nature of performance management and how an appraisal process fits into that concept. Obviously, not all performance will be good, and so now is the time discuss how to manage poor performance when it arises.

Imagine the situation where you've had an appraisal with someone and highlighted areas where you feel that their performance needed to improve, and after a couple of months there is no improvement. What do you do?

Each situation will have its individual circumstances, but there are some basic principles which you need to follow:

> Make sure the staff member is aware of what is expected of them. This could be by highlighting the relevant part of their job description, it could also be written down on their appraisal form, or it could be in written confirmation of an informal chat where you've raised any issues of concern. This could be as simple as an email.

> Ensure that adequate resources are available for them to do their job. Make sure they have been given enough time to meet deadlines, they have the appropriate tools (software, for example), and they have the appropriate information and team input.

> Check in with them. This might just be an informal 'how're you getting along?' but the aim is to head off any further problems before they get worse.

> Set a deadline or timeframe to have a more structured catch up meeting – this could be two weeks/four weeks/two months. There is no definitive correct timeframe. It will depend on what the issue is. There is little point in having a catch up meeting with someone when they haven't had the chance to show that they have understood the problem and been able to improve upon it. It may be a simple question of opportunity arising.

> Be sure that you can honestly say that you've done all you can to help them achieve the appropriate level of performance.

Only once you've ticked these boxes, should you be considering more formal action.

You may hear people refer to putting someone on a performance management plan or similar. What this entails, in reality, is following the steps above. They will have sat down with their employee, explained what is expected of them, made sure they understand what's expected of them and set a realistic timeframe for the expectations to be met. (This is another occasion where those SMART goals referenced in Chapter 5 come in useful.)

If, after all these steps have been followed, there is still no perceived or sufficient improvement, you might then decide to make use of the formal disciplinary procedure (see below).

HOW TO ADDRESS MISCONDUCT AND GROSS MISCONDUCT

Misconduct relates to some form of action and behaviour that is not acceptable in the workplace. More often than not you will have lists of examples in your disciplinary policy. There is no standard list of misconduct or gross misconduct, although you will find very similar examples in most companies. It's also possible to tell what issues a particular company has struggled with by what is listed in their examples.

It is highly unlikely that you will be able to list every possible misdemeanour that may arise within your company, so such lists should always be examples and not exhaustive.

Most issues are fairly obvious, as is the difference between misconduct and gross misconduct. As it suggests, gross misconduct is reserved for serious issues such as racism or theft or violence, but may also include matters that are serious to the specific company. For example, poor timekeeping may typically be considered to be misconduct, but in a company where keeping to a schedule is a key part of the service, such as Transport for London or an airline, poor timekeeping may be listed as gross misconduct.

TYPICAL EXAMPLES OF MISCONDUCT AND GROSS MISCONDUCT

Misconduct:

> **Bad timekeeping and/or lateness**

> **Unacceptable performance**

> **Insubordination**

> **Inappropriate standard of dress**

> **Smoking on company premises other than in authorised areas**

> **Contravention of minor safety regulations**

> **Disruptive behaviour**

> **Unauthorised or inappropriate use of the telephone or computer system.**

Gross misconduct:

> **Theft, fraud, falsification of records (including timesheets/ expense claims)**

> **Serious insubordination, e.g. refusing to carry out**

a reasonable management instruction

> **Violent, abusive or intimidating conduct**

> **Deliberate damage to company property**

> **Sexual, racial or other harassment or discrimination**

> **Unauthorised use or disclosure of confidential information**

> **Attending work under the influence of alcohol or illegal drugs**

> **Rudeness to clients or suppliers**

> **Bribery/accepting a gift without authorisation**

> **Prolonged unexplained absence**

> **Breach of company health and safety policy**

> **Conviction for a serious criminal offence.**

As with performance related issues, there is a general expectation that minor instances of misconduct would be addressed informally in the first instance.

Often, people don't seem to understand how others may view their actions or behaviour until it's pointed out to them. More cynically, it's possible that some people may have been pushing their luck, and when they realise that they haven't slipped under the radar, they will simply stop the inappropriate behaviour. It's equally true that you may have several informal chats with some people and they will still not realise the implications of their behaviour. In such instances, you may find that invoking the disciplinary procedure is necessary simply to get people to understand that you take these actions seriously.

2. THE DISCIPLINARY PROCESS

HOW AND WHEN TO USE THE DISCIPLINARY PROCESS

The phrase 'putting someone on a disciplinary', which you often hear being bandied around, is rather meaningless. Not to get too pedantic about it, you should not begin a formal disciplinary procedure until the time is right and you've pursued other possible avenues to address the problem.

It's worth remembering why the disciplinary process exists: it is a means whereby an employer can address instances of poor performance or misconduct in a structured manner. It isn't a cane to thrash recalcitrant employees with indiscriminately. It should always be used appropriately and in context.

The Advisory, Conciliation and Arbitration Service (ACAS) produces guidelines regarding both the disciplinary and grievance procedures. Although the ACAS guidelines are not legally binding, if you fail to follow the guidelines, you may still fall foul of an employment tribunal judge in their ruling. The guidelines are there for the purpose of providing fairness and consistency in the way that employees are treated.

📖 www.acas.org.uk/

Before you embark on the disciplinary process, remember the purpose!

The process may seem very formal and unfriendly, and it can be easy to get lost in the process. Never forget your original purpose: you are looking for certain behaviour or actions to change. Throughout the whole process, remain approachable and keep the lines of communication open. Just because you've started the process, doesn't mean that the end is inevitable. Be open to apologies or some level of contrition. Use the process rather than allowing it to become the driving force.

There are four basic stages of the disciplinary process: investigation; formal meeting; documented outcome; and appeal.

INVESTIGATION

You should never make any assumptions about a potential disciplinary matter until a thorough and objective investigation has taken place. The ACAS guidelines suggest that an independent party conducts the investigation if possible, which is why some smaller companies may choose to use an external consultant.

An investigation may take the form of interviewing witnesses to an incident and taking statements, or reviewing and printing off emails and other correspondence. Basically, this is the process of gathering evidence to help decide whether or not the matter should be taken further. If it is decided that there is a disciplinary issue to answer, then the employee should be provided with all the related evidence that you have used to make the decision.

DISCIPLINARY PROCEDURE

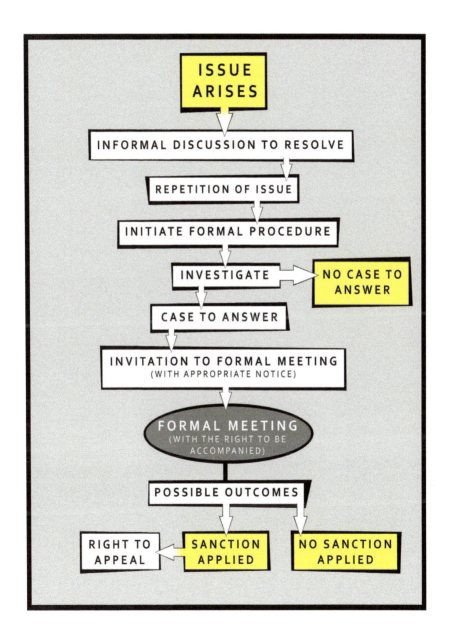

FORMAL MEETING

A formal meeting requires an invitation and reasonable notice, as well as notification of the right to be accompanied.

🅰 Invitation to disciplinary meeting letter

There is no specific legal requirement about the amount of notice that should be given, but a common guideline is that a minimum of 48 hours is reasonable. The point is to give the employee reasonable time in which to prepare. Obviously, if they have lots of documentation to read through and prepare a response to, this may take longer.

Each case will be judged on its own merits. The invitation itself should clearly state the reasons for the meeting, and not just something vague such as 'insubordination'. Be specific (e.g. 'you spoke loudly using inappropriate language to your manager which constitutes insubordination').

The meeting itself should enable the employee to give their side of the story. But you also need to be sure to manage the meeting and ensure that the main reason for the meeting is raised and discussed. We discuss certain difficult situations that may arise below.

You would not usually inform the employee of the outcome of the meeting immediately in the meeting itself. A period of reflection is advisable, even if it's only fifteen minutes or so. Be sure of your facts and reflect upon any business impact as the main driver behind your decision.

THE RIGHT TO BE ACCOMPANIED

Employees attending a formal meeting have the right to be accompanied by 'a fellow worker, a trade union official or a certified union representative' (Employment Relations Act 1999).

You have the right to refuse a parent, a friend who is studying law, a solicitor – assuming they do not fall into any of the categories above. You could also choose to accept the attendance of these individuals if you preferred.

It may seem daunting if an employee chooses to bring a union representative. Many creative companies are not unionised and so experience of dealing with unions is limited. In fact, union representatives are well-versed in the dos and don'ts of such meetings and it is sometimes easier to deal with them than with a well-intentioned colleague who may keep interrupting or speaking out of turn.

What is the role of the companion?

They can:

> Put forward or sum up the employee's case

> Respond on the employee's behalf to any view expressed at the meeting

> Confer with the employee

> Ask questions of any witness and address the meeting.

They cannot:

> Answer questions on behalf of the employee (but you may want to allow this if there are language barriers or if your employee is particularly upset or overawed).

TAKING NOTES

> Notes should always be taken in formal meetings. These serve to record the main points of what has been discussed and any action points agreed. Notes do not have to be word for word. Although you do need to keep the matter as confidential as possible, it is also almost impossible to run a meeting well and take notes at the same time, so ideally the note-taker will be someone other than the person taking the meeting. This is another instance where the use of external support may be a good option.

> There is an increasing use of voice recording devices in meetings. This has the advantage of accuracy, but will also need transcription. Covert recordings may be produced within an employment tribunal if the judge deems that they are 'relevant to the circumstances of a case'. The implication being that any notes of the meeting may be inaccurate or misleading in some way.

> If you follow good practice, this is unlikely to arise. Take notes, and ensure your employee has a copy. Ideally, you might ask your employee to sign the notes to show that they agree that they are an accurate reflection of the meeting. If they don't, they have the opportunity to give their version.

DOCUMENTED OUTCOME

It may be that, after the meeting, you agree with the employee's version of events and choose not to take the matter any further. You still need to confirm this in writing. If this means that another employee becomes involved in an investigation or disciplinary meeting, the first employee need not know that, or certainly need not know the details. Alternatively, you may decide that a sanction of some sort is warranted. Again, this needs to be confirmed in writing.

🅐 Outcome of disciplinary meeting letter

SANCTIONS

You may decide that there is no cause to take action after a formal meeting, but sometimes you may feel that a sanction of some sort is the most appropriate outcome.

Your options are:

> Verbal warning – although ACAS no longer recommends this as part of a formal procedure, it does occasionally serve its purpose in preventing a problem escalating

> First written warning –
  or an improvement notice
  (typically, remains live
  for six months)

> Final written warning –
  typically remains live
  for a year

> Dismissal – as
  discussed below.

APPEAL

Your employee will have the right to appeal against any sanction that you might choose to impose. Whoever conducts the appeal meeting should be different from and of equivalent status to the person taking the original disciplinary meeting. Often with small companies that can be difficult, so there is some leeway given depending on who may be available: another benefit of using external consultants, who also provide an additional level of objectivity to the situation.

The appeal process concludes the internal disciplinary procedure. Any further recourse by an employee would be external, for example via an employment tribunal.

ⓐ Invitation to appeal meeting letter
ⓐ Outcome of appeal meeting letter

3. THE OTHER SIDE OF THE COIN: THE GRIEVANCE PROCESS

Just as with the formal disciplinary procedure, the formal grievance procedure is for use if informal or other means have not been successful in resolving an issue. And as with the disciplinary procedure, the best recommendation is to use the ACAS guidelines.

Grievances can be regarded as the other side of the coin to 'disciplinaries'. The grievance procedure is a way in which an employee or worker can raise issues about which they feel aggrieved. Most often, if an employee has an issue of some sort, they will have a chat with someone or send an email about it, and the manager or HR representative will help to resolve it. In some cases, however, an employee may feel that the matter has not been resolved to their satisfaction and they may choose to raise a formal grievance. If this is the case, you do need to take it seriously.

WHAT DOES A GRIEVANCE LOOK LIKE?

> It should be written and could be in an email or letter.

> It could come about as a result of an appraisal meeting or an exit interview.

Grievances are typically related to working conditions (e.g. working hours, or pay) or working relationships with colleagues or others.

However, the grievance process is not intended to be a way that confrontational employees can get their own way or refuse to be appropriately managed. A manager does have the right to manage!

WHO SHOULD CONDUCT THE GRIEVANCE PROCESS?

Every company has to have in its written statements of terms and conditions the name or the title of the person that the staff can go to with any grievances. Consider carefully who this might be.

In smaller companies, you may have little choice because it will be expected to be a senior person. However, if a grievance is against a line manager or senior person, then obviously it would be inappropriate for them to conduct the process. It's also a good idea for the person conducting the process to be, shall we say, of a calm and unflustered nature. Unfortunately, grievances by their very nature can become quite personal or vitriolic towards the company. Listening to what is said calmly and objectively is part of the process.

To the person raising the grievance, it is often the case that the mere act of having the opportunity to give their views and say their piece out loud will go a long way to helping to resolve the situation. This is especially true if the complaint is about not being taken seriously or not being listened to.

As with disciplinary issues, sometimes it is good sense simply to be seen to be as objective as possible and engage external consultants in the grievance process – whether for the investigation alone, or also for any formal meetings. Certainly, smaller organisations may find themselves seeking external support for any appeals that may arise.

As with the disciplinary process, there are the four basic stages of the grievance process:

> **Investigation**: You need to know what the grievance is about. It is strongly suggested that part of the investigation process would be to meet with the person raising the grievance. You may also wish to offer them the right to be accompanied to the investigation meeting, even though it is not a formal meeting. This might seem an obvious point, but sometimes companies will conduct an investigation into the matters raised by an employee, then call the employee into a formal meeting in an effort to resolve the matter, and only then find out that there are additional issues about which they were unaware. Simply, make sure that the investigation is thorough and maintains a balance between confidentiality and ensuring that all sides of the story are reviewed.

> **Formal meeting**: Even if you feel that the grievance is unfounded after investigation, you should still hold a formal meeting with the team member who raised the grievance. This formal meeting is an intrinsic part of the ACAS guidelines. To fail to hold it would suggest you have not taken the matter sufficiently seriously. Just as with the disciplinary process (described above), you should issue a formal invitation with at least 48 hours' notice, including any documentary evidence you are going to use to reach a decision, and offering the employee the right to bring a companion to the meeting. It is very important that the employee has every opportunity during the meeting to raise all their complaints

CASE STUDY:
Parking problem gives rise to pay grievance

Following an increase in rail fares, an employee decided that it was cheaper and more practical to run a small car and drive to work than to use public transport. She tried to park in the car park to the rear of the office, but was told by the security guard that her company had no spaces there. She asked the MD for a space and was turned down. She raised a grievance because there were parking spaces available and she felt the company should be able to arrange for her to use one because it didn't pay her very much and so she had to use the cheapest form of transport to get to work.

In brief, the grievance was not upheld because:

> No one in the company had a parking space allocated and paid for

> There was nothing in the employee's terms and conditions of employment that suggested she was entitled to a parking space

> Public transport served the company and other workers well

> The employee's pay was in line with her peers

> There were no mitigating circumstances, such as a disability which might have altered the position.

and that this opportunity is noted. This ensures that you are seen to have addressed all the issues.

Ⓐ Invitation to grievance meeting letter

> **Documented outcome**: You should consider all that has been put before you and then decide if the grievance is upheld or not (i.e. whether you agree with the person raising the grievance or not). This decision should be recorded in a letter to the employee.

Ⓐ Outcome of grievance meeting letter

> **Appeal**: The team member has the right to appeal against the decision reached. This will be within a certain number of days (use the ACAS guidelines if you have no policy of your own) and to someone who was not involved in the original investigation and meeting. External consultants can support you if you have run out of senior staff members to conduct the appeal and hold the meeting. The appeal does need to set out specific grounds for disagreeing with the decision made. Once the appeal meeting has been held and a written response provided to the employee (e.g. based on the letter

used for a disciplinary appeal), that concludes the internal process.

COMMON PRINCIPLES FOR DISCIPLINARY AND GRIEVANCE PROCEDURES

Confidentiality – only involve those who are directly affected by the situation. Even fellow directors or senior staff need not know the details while the process is ongoing. Obviously, it does rather depend on each particular instance, but keep the principle of confidentiality in mind at all times. This relates to storage of notes and papers, as well as who knows what.

Documentation – keep a thorough record. Each stage should be documented and the paper trail filed safely. Recording, although initially rather off-putting, does at least ensure an accurate record. However good a note-taker is, the results will still be notes as opposed to a verbatim record.

Reasonableness – decisions that you make should be reasonable in light of the facts that you've been able to establish and given a balanced view of them. Any apparently arbitrary or irrational decisions will be viewed askance by an employment tribunal judge.

Consistency – consider how you have addressed similar cases in the past. Be sure that your actions show fairness in your dealings with all your staff.

FREQUENTLY ASKED QUESTIONS ABOUT DISCIPLINARY AND GRIEVANCE PROCEDURES

Q. What happens if someone makes a complaint, but won't raise a formal grievance and doesn't want their name mentioned?
A. Explain that this will hinder your ability to make a thorough investigation and try to find out why they don't wish to be involved by name. It may be that they feel bullied or harassed so this is a form of self-preservation, or it may be that they have some kind of grudge and are merely making trouble. Ultimately, if someone does not wish to be named, you cannot force them, but in some respects this will make their evidence less strong.

Q. What happens if you invite someone to a disciplinary meeting and they then raise a grievance against you?
A. The act of inviting someone to a disciplinary meeting is not in itself sufficient reason to raise a legitimate grievance. However, if the grievance has some other wider basis it will need to be addressed by someone other than you. If the disciplinary matter and grievance subject are connected, the two processes may be able to proceed in parallel. However, if the grievance matter is separate, the disciplinary process should be put on hold pending the outcome of the grievance.

Q. What happens if you invite someone to a disciplinary meeting and then they are signed off with stress for a month?
A. This can sometimes be used as a delaying tactic, but equally can be a valid and genuine problem. Allow them time to recover fully, ensuring

that their absence is fully covered by a Statement of Fitness for Work or 'fit note'. Don't badger them while they are off work. When they return to work, with the appropriate note indicating their fitness to do so, you can recommence the process.

Q. What happens if someone raises a grievance, it is found to have no grounds, but they still refuse to work with the person about whom they raised the grievance?
A. Be sure that the grievance procedure was followed properly, including a thorough and objective investigation. Try mediation. Discuss the situation with them and perhaps consider changes to their working pattern or conditions if possible. But ultimately you may be in a position where using the disciplinary procedure is an option. Refusing a reasonable management instruction can be deemed to be insubordination.

In certain serious instances, a possible outcome of a disciplinary or grievance procedure might be dismissal.

4. DEPARTING EMPLOYEES

This part of the chapter focuses on that often challenging time when one or a number of people leave your company. Remember that this is another one of those occasions when your actions will be under the microscope and subject to the rumour mill.

Whether the departure is your choice or their choice, whether you are dancing with glee that a particularly tricky employee has decided to resign or whether you have agonised over

making a valued employee redundant, you will be judged. And this judgement will affect your brand as an employer.

There are three principal ways in which staff may leave your company: dismissal, redundancy; and resignation.

You'll notice that the first two will be your decision, whereas the third is the decision of the staff member.

In each case, do not forget to follow the proper process. Let's take each instance in turn.

DISMISSAL

The implication here is that some kind of misconduct or poor performance has taken place and you've gone through the process of addressing it informally, but it has been repeated or another instance has arisen or the performance hasn't improved.

So, you have done all you can to rectify the situation. You've given your staff member clear guidance, adequate resources and the opportunity to improve or change. You've implemented the formal disciplinary procedure and have worked your way through the various sanctions, or have found that the single instance of misdemeanour is so serious that you have made the decision to dismiss your employee.

You do need to be absolutely sure this is the right option. It is a huge responsibility to deprive someone of their livelihood.

If you dismiss an employee, having gone through the appropriate process, you will of course confirm this in writing, and should give the reason for the dismissal.

LEGITIMATE REASONS FOR DISMISSAL

In order for dismissal to be fair, it must be for one of five specific reasons:

> Capability – you've gone through the performance management process and your employee is still unable to fulfil their duties to an appropriate standard; or perhaps one of your staff has a long-term illness, you've done all you can to support them and give them a chance to recover, but they remain unable to work.

> Conduct – you've gone through the disciplinary procedure and found your employee is guilty of repeated misconduct or maybe one instance of gross misconduct.

> Illegality or contravention of a statutory duty – for instance, a driver loses their licence.

> Some other substantial reason e.g. an employee is sent to prison - this is something of a catch-all, but still requires a proper dismissal process to have been followed

> Redundancy – this is discussed separately below.

DISMISSAL FOR POOR PERFORMANCE

> Be certain that the person is aware that their performance is not acceptable. Provide them with a job description and a clear explanation of your expectations.

> Discuss what 'good' performance looks like and any deliverables that are needed.

> Ensure that they are aware of the potential outcome if their performance does not improve. E.g. 'We may put in place a performance management plan.'

> If the performance management plan is exhausted unsuccessfully, explain the disciplinary process and potential outcome.

DISMISSAL FOR MISCONDUCT AND GROSS MISCONDUCT

> Ensure that the staff member is aware that their action or behaviour constitutes misconduct.

> Make sure that they know what the potential repercussions may be. E.g. implementation of the disciplinary process, with possible sanctions up to and including dismissal.

> Tell the person what the impact of their behaviour or action is on the business and their colleagues – so not just 'your timekeeping is poor, do better', but 'your timekeeping is poor and this has an impact on your colleagues because they have to cover for you and their tasks suffer as a result, this means that our service to our clients is not as good as it should be'.

REDUNDANCY

I'm sure it will come as no surprise that ACAS has guidelines for redundancy which you should follow.

Redundancy must be for legitimate reasons, namely: the closure of a business or workplace, or changes in the workplace that mean that fewer employees are needed. Many of us experienced redundancy during the recent economic crisis. Indeed, the architecture profession has probably had more significant experience of this process than most.

It seems commonly viewed that the redundancy process itself is too long and drawn out, and has negative effects on all those involved. (You may hear: 'People don't like to be kept hanging around'; 'It has such a negative effect on morale that no work gets done while the consultation period is going on.') For that reason, some companies try to cut it short, risking claims from disgruntled employees. However good the intentions, if you don't follow the process – including having a meaningful consultation period – then you (the company) are automatically in the wrong.

The challenge during redundancy, as with the disciplinary process, is to balance getting the process right with retaining your sensitivity.

Ironically, given the prevalence of redundancy in the past few years, people are more used to the process and understand that it isn't just some sadistic series of events dreamt up by the HR department to keep themselves in a job. There is a logic to the process, in that companies should not be able to simply implement cuts in staff numbers without input from those who may be affected. There should be the opportunity for people to offer to work fewer hours, or take a pay cut for a period of time. These options have certainly worked to stave off compulsory redundancies in some cases over the past few years.

The key points of the redundancy procedure are:

> **Planning**: Basically, how to avoid compulsory redundancies (e.g. perhaps by implementing reduced hours or salary cuts).

> **Identifying the pool for selection**: This will be those doing similar work or in a particular department where there is over-capacity or where finances cannot support the existing numbers; a poorly planned pool will automatically make the whole process unfair.

> **Seeking volunteers**: It is good practice to offer a voluntary redundancy package, which may minimise compulsory redundancies.

> **Consulting employees**: This is a legal requirement: the timing will vary depending on the number of likely redundancies; the consultation must be meaningful.

> **Selection for redundancy**: This must be accomplished using objective criteria such as performance or skills.

> **Appeals and dismissals**: A formal meeting and notice of dismissal, including the right to appeal the decision must be part of the process.

> **Suitable alternative employment**: Continue to offer opportunities if they arise.

> **Redundancy payment**: Statutory amounts apply and you can choose to offer more if you wish and have the ability to do so.

> **Counselling and support**: Again, it's good practice to do what you can, even if it's as simple as helping with CVs or offering the contact details of recruitment agencies.

If you believe you may have to make redundancies, do involve your staff in the process. If you explain the challenges that you face, you may be surprised at the sacrifices that people are prepared to make to support the business. It's another of those instances where, if you engage people and make them feel part of the decision-making process, they will usually act in the best way for the business.

SURVIVORS' GUILT

This is now a recognised phenomenon. Those who remain in a company after a redundancy process can feel guilty because they've seen friends and colleagues leave against their will and they are left behind.

Just as those leaving may need support, so may those who remain. Giving people some leeway to, in effect, mourn the loss of their team mates will help you to return to an effective workplace more quickly.

RESIGNATION

In this case, the choice is taken out of your hands. Sometimes, a resignation will be welcome; sometimes it's bad news and you may ask the staff member to reconsider.

In any event, it is always good practice and a useful experience to hold exit interviews with the team member.

The reasons for leaving may be personal and something that you can do nothing about such as relocation, childcare or health. If that's the case, you can still ask a departing employee some useful questions about their working experience in your company.

If the reasons are more career orientated or related to problems at work, you have the opportunity to do something about it.

5. EXIT INTERVIEWS

Exit interviews should be carried out with all departing employees: you can always learn something. Conduct the interview in the office in a meeting room if possible (i.e. not just down the pub or over lunch). This indicates that it is an important process to you, not just a bit of a chat. You can always take the person to lunch or for a leaving drink in addition.

Be sure to ask the same questions of each person who leaves, so that you have comparable information.

EXIT INTERVIEW QUESTIONS

Begin with addressing the basic purpose behind holding an exit interview:

> What is your reason for leaving?

> What has been positive for you in your time with us?

> What has been frustrating/difficult/upsetting to you in your time with us?

You can then ask other questions regarding specific elements of their working time with you. For example:

> How well do you think your development needs were assessed and met?

> Did your experience in the company meet with your expectations?

> What improvements could be made to the recruitment/induction process?

> How well were you managed during your time with the company?

> What suggestions would you make to improve working conditions, hours, etc.?

> How could the organisation reduce stress levels among employees?

You may want to find out about their future plans:

> Are you happy to say where you are going (if you have decided)?

> What is the attraction of working for them?

> What, importantly, are they offering that we are not?

> (If appropriate) Could you be persuaded to discuss the possibility of staying?

> Would you consider working for us again in the future if the situation was right?

A good catch-all question is: 'Is there anything else that it might be useful for me to know that might help other people in the future?'

You may feel justified in being annoyed or resentful because a valued employee is leaving – especially someone who you've spent time and money on developing and who you saw as a part of the future of your company. I'm aware of individuals receiving calls from senior management and their wives expressing anger and betrayal, and trying to engender a feeling of guilt for resigning. This does not leave a positive image and can damage a company's reputation. The best thing to do is to put a brave face on it, wish them well and say that they would always be welcomed back if an opportunity existed.

And, it does happen. The grass is not always greener. And people's circumstances change.

RESIGNATION

EMPLOYEE DECIDES TO LEAVE

RESIGNATION SUBMITTED

EXIT INTERVIEW

PERSONAL REASONS

WORK RELATED

EMPLOYER CANNOT AFFECT

EMPLOYER CAN AFFECT

RESIGNATION ACCEPTED

CHANGES NOT POSSIBLE / NOT APPROPRIATE

CHANGES MADE

DEPARTURE

DEPARTURE

RESIGNATION WITHDRAWN

EMPLOYEE STAYS

6. RETURN

Back in 1961 Charlie Drake had a surprise hit with a novelty song 'My boomerang won't come back'. I couldn't help but think of it when I managed a Boomerang Programme which catered for people returning to the company having left and spent time elsewhere.

Despite the association of the song and, indeed, the 'throwing weapon' itself, the concept of celebrating someone's welcome return to your company is a good one.

The ideal situation would be that they were a model employee who you were sad to lose, but who went away and gained all sorts of useful experience elsewhere at someone else's expense, which they are now bringing back to the benefit of you and your company. It's the scenario described above (and which worries you when you pay for people to go on expensive training courses).

However, in this new enlightened age where you treat your employees like adults and give them the freedom to learn and take control of their own professional development, this is the sort of thing that may happen. And, just as you may gain by it on one hand, you may lose by it on the other.

People vote with their feet and will move on to work at a company whose management style and business ethics match their own beliefs and values. This personal alignment with work is increasingly obvious within the workplace.

MAKING THE MOST OF RETURNING EMPLOYEES

> **Let people know:** Obviously let your staff know, but also let your clients and contacts know.

> **Welcome them properly:** Don't ignore your orientation process and assume they already know everything. Times will have changed since they were last with you.

> **Respect their new status:** Even if they left you as a newly qualified graduate and it's only six months or a year later, they will have gained increased experience and value to bring to your company.

> **Educate your staff:** Be sure that your staff know what additional skills and expertise the person is bringing back to the company. The same applies to any recruit, new or returning, of course, but be sure not to assume you and everyone else knows what they have to offer.

> **Celebrate the return:** Don't be shy, it's kudos to you and the company that this person wants to come back. You don't have to go mad, but perhaps drinks or cakes in the office will serve to mark the occasion.

SUMMARY: DEPARTURE AND RETURN

Not all departures from your company are necessarily bad.

Don't be bitter or vindictive when someone chooses to leave you. Aside from it being unprofessional and sometimes childish, it is more profitable to learn from the experience. See if there are any changes you can put in place to prevent the people you want to keep from leaving in the future.

If you are the one making the decision for the person to leave, be sure to follow the proper procedure so that you remain within the law, but also don't forget that you are dealing with people and don't lose your sensitivity to their situation. Even if they have committed a heinous act of gross misconduct, they have the right to understand the business impact of what they have done and that this is the driver behind your decision. Don't make it personal or vitriolic or engage in pointless verbal or written slanging matches. Help them to learn from the experience so that they don't do it again.

CONCLUSION

The previous chapters should have helped you to become significantly more confident in understanding how the different elements of HR fit together to work to the benefit of your practice. It is clear that prevention is preferable to cure when it comes to people and people management. Above all, nothing can beat common sense and communication.

SOME THOUGHTS ABOUT THE FUTURE

There remains an air of 'let's wait and see' about the market. However, at the time of writing employees are generally more positive about prospects. They are scanning the jobs market to see what new and better paid opportunities may be out there, particularly because many may not have seen an increase in salary for a while – some have even seen their salaries reduce. As a consequence, companies that have some great new projects and are in a position to outbid their competitors for the highest quality candidates may benefit. Alternatively, employees may present their current employer with an offer of employment elsewhere which is then counter-offered by their present employer – therefore increasing the employee's salary without the risk of starting again in a new and different environment. Equally, employees who feel they were ill-treated by their employers during the recession may take the chance of a more positive climate to move on.

As with previous recessions, architects and designers will have left the profession and will be working in a new career or may have left the country in search of work. The long-lasting effect of this will be a skills gap and a dearth of high-quality candidates to go around in our creative companies. A recruitment agency recently told me: 'As a candidate you can't get fulfilling work in your chosen design practice; and as an office you can't find the calibre of staff – which in essence means you get compromises'. The market may have picked up with some level of enthusiasm, but now companies are realising that it's not as it was and they are faced with a range of new challenges. As the agent put it: 'It's like being a cheese lover but all you can get is Kraft triangles.'

Putting enlightened HR practices into place will help you to face these challenges.

DRAWING IT ALL TOGETHER

I am not advocating that all companies should have an HR manager, but certainly someone with some basic HR knowledge should assume responsibility for the function. This book will at least provide you with that basic knowledge and will ensure that you are aware of when you may need to seek greater expertise.

When you are approaching an HR or a people-related matter be sure to use the best information resources.

The seminal sources for employment legislation and people-related matters are:

💻 www.acas.org.uk
💻 www.gov.uk

If you are in any doubt about points of law, check on these sites. They will always be the most up-to-date sources of information.

You may find other information via a search engine, but you can never be sure if it is current – or indeed if it relates to the UK. I have on several occasions been challenged about a change to legislation or questioned about a business practice, only to discover that the original query came from a Canadian website or an article written about working life in the United Arab Emirates.

If in doubt, seek advice from an HR professional or employment lawyer. Use common sense and treat all staff consistently and fairly, and you can't go far wrong. Firefighting is rarely the best option.

IT'S ALL FINE UNTIL IT ISN'T – CAUTIONARY TALES FROM THE HR ARCHIVE

> **Three university friends started their design practice together and built a successful business. They worked well together and their work and personal lives blended in a natural way. Then one of the founders seemed to change. Let's call her Sue. Sue was unfocused at work, came in late, worked from home a lot. She seemed terse with the staff and dismissive with her fellow partners. Eventually, the other two partners faced the fact that they had to address this somehow. They concluded early on that they had no real idea how to deal with the situation aside from having a**

chat with Sue. They did and she denied any change in her behaviour, any problems at work or at home, told them they were making it up and even implied that they were picking on her because she was female. They realised they needed help and support from an HR professional.

> Paul was hired by a small practice as a senior architect. His CV and portfolio indicated such excellent skills and experience that the practice was grateful just to have someone to let loose on one of their key projects. After a few months, feedback from the client wasn't good. The partners took a closer look at his work and realised there were some problems. They took him aside and raised the issues with him. Paul made it clear that as far as he was concerned he was doing a good job. His way of working had been perfectly fine for his previous employer. Anyway, he didn't have a job description so how was he supposed to know exactly what was expected of him? He felt they were bullying him unfairly. Eventually his attitude led one of the directors to lose his temper and suggest to Paul that he might be better off employed elsewhere. Paul walked out of the office and next day sent in a sick note signing him off work with stress. The partners realised they needed professional HR help to resolve the situation.

The benefits of enlightened HR practice:

> Saves time and therefore money
> Minimises risk of claims and fines
> Clarifies company ethos and culture
> Attracts professional staff through professional environment and standards
> Retains staff, giving them clear career progression opportunities through clarity of process.

The disadvantages of bad HR practice:

> Is restrictive
> Focuses on what you can't do rather than what you can do
> Is process driven
> Lacks flexibility
> Is commercially unaware.

WHY SHOULD THE ARCHITECTURE PROFESSION SUPPORT HR WITHIN THEIR PRACTICE STRUCTURE?

You entered the profession to make a positive impact on the built environment. Your focus may be design, or technical matters, or job running. This is your speciality and skill.

Why would you want to spend your precious time focusing on something about which you know only a little, you don't enjoy and with which you do not feel confident? Doesn't it make sense to seek an expert to carry out what is necessary?

As a practice owner, partner, director or manager, you can't completely

devolve responsibility for HR, but you can certainly delegate the routine administrative elements, and seek and follow the input of your chosen HR professional. This will allow you to focus on what you are good at and enjoy, and enable the HR person to do the same.

HR professionals like addressing issues before they become a problem. Following the proper process is second nature to us. We just need your support to do our jobs properly.

Please don't wait until a problem has arisen before you tell us. We can get rid of the mole hills before they become mountains. Treat us with respect as fellow professionals and we can support you, advise you, watch your back, protect you from most risk, and help you to gain and keep a reputation as a caring, sharing employer of choice!

THE FUTURE OF HR

The future of HR is bright. We are finally beginning to be taken seriously as a profession. It is a massive step forward that HR and employment practice is now often a part of the professional practice curriculum in many schools of architecture. The shame is that it is not compulsory. I still do not understand why, in a profession where people – what is in their heads and what they can contribute – are an essential part of the unique nature of each company, it is the people elements of the business are often secondary to IT and far far behind finance. It would be unrealistic for financial concerns to be ignored in favour of people; a business has to make money. However, aren't people as important as money and machines to the success of your practice?

HR is moving from a simple administrative function to having the ability to make a significant positive impact on your business. Think about the models that were mentioned in Chapter 2. Although the ability to maintain accurate records, focus on detail and manage acres of paperwork is a skill in itself, nevertheless increased value lies in enhancing your reputation in the marketplace through improving employee retention and reward, involvement with local universities, and community outreach – among other initiatives.

You want to be better than your competition. You want to be an attractive and engaging place to work. You would like to give something back to the profession and to society.

HR is in a prime position to help you do that. We walk and talk with your people; we listen, we solve problems, we make suggestions for improvement or offer innovative ideas to make your employees happier, healthier and so more effective and efficient.

The future has to be about the architecture profession and HR profession working together to the benefit of both.

BIBLIOGRAPHY

GENERAL REFERENCE

Armstrong M and Taylor S (2014). *Armstrong's Handbook of Human Resource Management Practice*, 13th edition, Kogan Page.

Torrington D, Hall L and Taylor S (2009). *Fundamentals of Human Resource Management: Managing People at Work*, FT Prentice Hall.

Torrington D, Taylor S and Hall L (2011). *Human Resource Management*, FT Prentice Hall.

Truss C, Mankin D and Kelliher C (2012). *Strategic Human Resource Management*, Oxford University Press.

Walton J (1999). *Strategic Human Resource Development*, FT Prentice Hall.

MANAGING CREATIVITY AND/OR INTERNATIONALLY

Bartlett CA and Ghoshal S (2002). *Managing Across Borders: The Transnational Solution*, Harvard Business School Press.

Buckingham M and Coffman C (1999). *First, Break All the Rules: What the World's Greatest Managers Do Differently*, Simon & Schuster.

Goleman D (1998). *Working With Emotional Intelligence*, Bloomsbury.

Hofstede G, Hofstede GJ and Minkov M (2010). *Cultures and Organizations: Software of the Mind: Intercultural Cooperation and Its Importance for Survival*, McGraw-Hill Professional.

MacKenzie G (1998). *Orbiting the Giant Hairball: A Corporate Fool's Guide to Surviving with Grace*, Viking/Allen Lane.

Maister D (2003). *Managing the Professional Service Firm*, Freepress.

Marston C (2010). *Generational Insights*, Cam Marston.

Pascale R (1990). *Managing on the Edge: How Successful Companies Use Conflict to Stay Ahead*, Penguin.

Trompenaars F and Hampden Turner C (1997). *Riding the Waves of Culture: Understanding Cultural Diversity in Business*, Nicholas Brealey Publishing.

ARTICLES

Aguinis H, Joo H, and Gottfredson RK (2013). 'What monetary rewards can and cannot do: How to show employees the money', *Business Horizons*, March.

Amabile TM and Khaire M (2008). 'Creativity and the role of the leader', *Harvard Business Review*, October.

Auger P et al (2013). 'How much does a company's reputation matter in recruiting?', *MIT Sloan Management Review*, Spring.

Buckingham M (2012). 'Leadership development in the age of the algorithm', *Harvard Business Review*, June.

Bunker KA, Kram KE and Ting S (2002). 'The young and the clueless', *HBR OnPoint*, December.

Cable DM, Gino F and Staats BR (2013). 'Reinventing employee onboarding', *MIT Sloan Management Review*, Spring.

Erickson TJ and Gratton L (2007). 'What it means to work here', *Harvard Business Review*, March.

Gabarro JJ and Hill LA (2002). 'Managing performance', Harvard Business School Background Note 496-022, October 1995. (Revised January 2002.), January 8.

Goffee R and Jones G (2007). 'Leading clever people', *Harvard Business Review*, March.

Hewlett SA, Sherbin L and Sumberg K (2009) 'How Gen Y & Boomers will reshape your agenda', *Harvard Business Review*, July–August.

Hinkin TR and Schriescheim CA (2009). 'Performance incentives for tough times', *Harvard Business Review*, March.

APPENDICES

1. APPLICATION FORM

[The company] believes strongly in the promotion of equal opportunities and will consider all applicants by the same criteria with reference to experience, academic achievements and other relevant skills required for the job. No applicant will be discriminated against on the grounds of race, religion or belief, sex, age, gender reassignment, marriage or civil partnership, pregnancy or maternity, sexual orientation or disability.

Offers of employment are contingent upon proof of identity and authorisation to work in the United Kingdom. Continued employment will be contingent upon having permission to work in the United Kingdom under the immigration rules, if applicable. [The company] reserves the right to implement the disciplinary process if proof of such is not provided.

General information	
Name:	Date:
Home address:	
Home no:	Mobile no:
Position desired:	Department:
Desired annual salary:	Earliest start date:

Employment authorisation
If your application is successful, can you verify that you have the right to work in the UK? YES / NO

References (Please provide details of three references, preferably business related. Please indicate any you would not like to be contacted unless you are employed)

Name, company and relationship	Email	Phone
1.		
2.		
3.		

Education (Most recent first)

Name of establishment	From–to	Subjects	Qualifications
1.			
2.			
3.			

Employment record (Most recent first. Cover the past 10 years if possible)

Employer:	From:		To:
Position held:	Salary:		
Description of duties:			
Reason for leaving:			
Employer:	From:		To:
Position held:	Salary:		
Description of duties:			
Reason for leaving:			

Professional memberships, registration, certification, etc:

Community organisations and activities:

Additional remarks:

Verification: Please sign below to confirm the following:
I confirm that I am able to perform all the essential functions of the job that I am applying for and I am able to meet the attendance requirements of this position. (If you are unable to do so, please describe any reasonable adjustments which could be made to enable you to perform this job.)

I hereby certify the accuracy of the information provided here and on my accompanying curriculum vitae and I give my permission for my references, except as noted, to be contacted in connection with this application.
I understand that providing false information may be grounds for termination of employment.

	Date:
Signature: _____	_____

OFFICE USE ONLY

Date of interview:	Interviewed by:	
Employed as:	Annual salary:	Start date:

2. INTERVIEW FORM

This form serves as a record of the interview and enables interviewers to make an assessment of the candidate's interview performance. It also provides a consistent approach to all candidates. Keep these records for at least two years.

During the interview score the candidate against each criterion. The total score can help to determine the candidate's suitability compared with others. The candidate may feel nervous if they realise that they are being scored and so it is advisable to record scores directly after the interview takes place, not during. Please note: the bullet points in each criterion are intended as a guide only.

Under the Data Protection Act, candidates are allowed to see this information and this should be borne in mind when completing the form.

Name of interviewer(s):	Date:
Name of interviewee:	Job title and department

Criterion Selection criteria examples	Comments Please remain factual and non-biased or non-discriminatory	Score 1 = poor 5 = excellent
Past experience: Previous role's relevance Responsibilities Scope of work Pace of work		
Knowledge: Company Industry Career Procedures		
Suitability for role: Commitment Enthusiasm Education Skills Knowledge of role		

Perceived ability to perform: Confidence Assertiveness Competence Determination		
Personality: Professionalism Clarity of thought Interaction Demeanour Body language		
Ambition: Long-term goals Strategic thinking Ultimate career direction		
Overall suitability Top score =		

3. INTERVIEW QUESTIONS

ROLE: PROJECT MANAGER

Quality/ability sought	Questions (using portfolio if appropriate)
Experience	Describe your role on this project.
Problem solving	What was your most difficult project experience?
	How did you approach it?
	Why this approach?
	What did you learn?
	What would you do differently next time?
Motivation/drivers	Tell me about your idea of success. (Meeting client needs? Winning an award?)
	Describe your most successful project.
	Why was it so successful?
	What did you enjoy most about this project?
Knowledge of PM 'process'	Why is the PM role important?
	Describe an ideal PM. Describe a poor one.
Financial management	What tools do you use to control projects?
	How do you manage the project schedule? how do you manage the fees?
	Can you show me any examples?
	How do you know if you are making a profit?
	What is a good profit?
	How does the company make money?
	How could it make more?
	If you could do one thing on a team to make it more profitable what would it be?
Interpersonal skills	How would your team describe you as a project manager?
	How would your client describe you as a project manager?
	How would senior management in your current company describe you as a project manager?
Client relationships	Tell me about the most difficult client you have ever had.
	Why so difficult?
	How did you deal with them?
Teams	Describe the best team you ever worked with.
	Why was it so successful?

ROLE: DESIGNER

Quality/ability sought	Questions (using portfolio if appropriate)
Work preference and experience	What type of work do you like to do?
	Why?
	How do you prefer to develop your design?
	How did you learn this way?
	Why do you prefer it?
Finding truth in the portfolio	What was your role on this project?
	What is the design concept?
	Pretend I am the client and sell it to me.
	Where were you when this design concept occurred to you?
Sales/communication	Pretend I am the client and I want to change this (granite to solid wood) – convince me otherwise.
	Define successful design. (Meeting budget? Meeting client's needs?)
Verbal skills and resourcing	How do you ascertain the client goals? Programme, aesthetic, budget …
Technical proficiency	Are these drawings yours? (Maybe too direct!)
	Were there any 'technical' issues with this design (roof leak, etc.)?
	What was the worst design you have ever seen?
	Why?
	How would you amend it?
Passion/communication	What would you change here (point to something)?
	Does the design work?
	Do you like it?
	Why?
	If fee were no object what would you have done differently on this?
	Why?

ROLE: INTERIOR DESIGNER

Quality/ability sought	Questions (using portfolio if appropriate)
Space planning	Ask about specific projects shown.
	Programming issues? Examples?
Goal setting	What were the goals in this project?
	Describe how you met the goals?
	What were the client goals? team goals? your goals?
Knowledge of furniture/ finishes	What were the design challenges?
	How did you solve them?
Budgets	What was the budget on this project?
	How do you track it?
	Do you think the budget really matters if the client likes the project in the end?
Specifications	Did you specify this furniture?
	Why?
	What was the procurement process on this project?
	What is the worst specification error you've ever seen made?
Presentation skills	'Present' your portfolio to me as a project.
	Pretend I am the client and I don't like what you just showed me – convince me that it is good.
Creativity/articulation	Describe a design to me that I can't see – using words only...
Drawing/rendering/ graphics	What tools do you use to communicate design intent?
	What works best?
	Why?

ROLE: PROJECT ARCHITECT/ARCHITECTURAL TECHNICIAN/CAD PRODUCTION

Quality/ability sought	Questions (using portfolio if appropriate)
CAD	Which software packages do you know?
	Which do you prefer and why?
	Which software is most effective for design?
	Why?
	Which software is the easiest/most difficult to use?
	If you could change it what would you change or make easier?
	Would you mind taking a test? (What is their reaction?)
	How long have you used CAD?
	Can you show me any examples?
	Why have you chosen these examples?
Site experience	What is the most interesting challenge you've ever had on site?
	How did you resolve it?
	Most difficult experience?
	How did you resolve it?
	Why is your role important?
	If you saw a potentially dangerous site condition, would you tell the contractor how to resolve it?
	What would you do?
Types of project	Ask for specific information on projects shown.
	What were the challenges on this project?
	What was different about it?
Problem solving	Obstacles?
	On time?
	On budget?
	What is special about this project?
	What would you do differently next time?
	Best/favourite project?
	Why was it the best?
	What was your specific role?
Consultant coordination	Who did ... on this project?
Relationships/communication	Most difficult consultant and why (without mentioning name – merely checking communication and conflict resolution skills) – how did you deal with him/her?

4. INDUCTION CHECKLIST

Employee's name:	Position:
Inductor's name:	Position:

Organisation	Check	Finance	Check
Introduction to key staff and team		Timesheet procedure	
Right to work in UK docs received		Overtime procedure	
Induction pack issued		Date and method of salary payment	
Handbook issued		Holiday and sick pay entitlement	
Company history		P45 received	
Mission statement		Expenses procedure	
Company overview and structure		Bank details received	
Telephone extension no. issued			
Business card issued		**Benefits**	Check
Login details issued		Pension scheme	
		Training scheme	
Health and safety	Check	Health insurance	
Work area risk assessment		Any other benefits	
Evacuation procedure			
Health and safety officer		**Housekeeping**	Check
First aiders and fire wardens		IT support	
Accident procedure		Stationery procedure	
		Company template location	
Company procedures	Check	Social functions (i.e. teambuilding)	
Appraisal procedure		Dress code	
Training policy		Smoking area	
Disciplinary and grievance policy		Refreshment facilities	
Probationary and notice period		Postal procedure	
Email and internet policy		Key areas (canteen, toilets etc.)	
Sickness/absence policy		Paper recycling	
Employee handbook		Carbon emission awareness	

Once all checked, please sign and date.

Employee's signature: _____ Date: _____

Inductor's signature: _____

5. PERSONAL DETAILS FORM

Please complete the following information and hand it to your inductor on your first day of employment.

This information is for administration purposes only. It will not be passed on to any third parties and will be used in accordance with the Data Protection Act (1998).

Personal information	
Full name:	Start date:
Job title:	Department:
Sex (please circle): Male Female	Marital status:
Date of birth:	Email address:
Home address:	
Home phone no:	Mobile phone no:
Doctor's details	
Doctor's name:	Name of surgery:
Address:	
Phone no:	
Emergency contacts	
Name:	Name:
Relationship:	Relationship:
Address:	Address:
Home phone no:	Home phone no:
Work phone no:	Work phone no:
Mobile phone no:	Mobile phone no:
Medical details	
If you have any medical conditions which, left untreated, may lead you to feel unwell, please document here. You do not have to disclose this information if you do not wish but it is advisable to in the event of you feeling unwell while at work:	

continued overleaf ····⁖

Bank / Tax details	
Name of bank or building society: Branch address:	

Name on account:	
Sort code:	Account no:
National Insurance no:	Payroll no (office use only):

Ethnic monitoring

Please circle one of the following. If you would rather not say, please leave blank:

White British	Black British African	Indian other
White Irish	Black British Caribbean	Chinese
White other	Black British other	Japanese
Black African	Indian	Oriental other
Black Caribbean	Pakistani	Mixed
Black other	Bangladeshi	Other ethnic background

Office use only

P45 obtained and filed?	Proof of right to work in UK copied and filed?	CV and signed contract filed?

6. APPRAISAL FORM

Appraisee name:	Position:	Department:
Appraiser 1 name:	Appraiser 2 name:	Date:

Achievements since last review
Please list up to three achievements since your last review:

1
2
3

Personal attributes
Please score yourself against the following criteria and comment on any or all areas if you desire:
1 = Improvement needed / 2 = Meets expectations
3 = Exceeds expectations / 4 = Exceptional ability

Criteria	Your score	Assessor's score	Comments
Planning, organising, initiative How goals are achieved, work planned, time managed, problem-solving abilities.			
Motivation Willingness to do the job, attitude to work, self motivation abilities.			
Confidentiality Recognise when discretion and tact are necessary.			
Team working Pro-actively supports colleagues, flexibility to task in hand and works jointly towards team objectives.			
Dependability/reliability Level of supervision required, attendance and punctuality record.			
Communication and interpersonal skills Promote good work relationships, able to put across ideas in a positive manner to achieve agreement.			
Managing others (if applicable) Ability to motivate, delegate, mentor, make decisions, communicate with team.			

continued overleaf ⋯⋗

Challenges faced over the last 12 months

Challenges	If you managed to overcome these challenges, tell us how. If not, tell us how the situation could have been avoided/improved upon

Personal development plan

Appraisee's career aspirations	
Short term	Medium/long-term

Key training and objectives for the next 12 months

Agreed training	Timescale
1	
2	
3	
Agreed objectives	Timescale
1	
2	
3	

Additional comments:

Appraisee's signature: _____

Appraiser 1 signature: _____

Appraiser 2 signature: _____

7. SMART GOALS WORKSHEET

Category (taken from appraisal form or general topic)	Task or action or objective (Be as specific as possible to ease clarity.)	Success measures (How are you going to know if the goal is achieved?)	Understood and clear (Are you sure that all parties are sure and agree about what is expected?)	Realistic (Is the goal achievable? Does the person have the time and resources to do it?)	Timeframe (What is the timeframe within which this goal will be actioned? Be specific.)
Example: Finance	Submit payroll report on time	Payroll will be submitted by 28th of each month	Submission means email sent and acknowledgement received from recipient	Staff member to confirm receipt of leaves of absence report/holiday report by 15th of each month in order to process payroll	Next payroll onwards – 28 January 2016
Business development	Develop networking skills and increase personal network connections	Meet two new industry connections each month and add to personal CRM	Engage two new connections in communication at an industry event and obtain their business cards	Choose industry events that will be well represented and where meeting two new people is realistic	Within 1 month/ each month

8. INVITATION TO DISCIPLINARY MEETING

[Date]
[Employee name],
[Address]

Dear [Employee name]

We met on [date] as part of the investigation into [add details of incident or allegations]. You were unable to provide a satisfactory explanation for this and so you are required to attend a disciplinary hearing on [insert date] at [insert time] in [insert location], in accordance with the organisation's disciplinary procedure. A copy of the disciplinary procedure is attached to this letter for your information.

I will chair the meeting and in attendance will be [name] and [name] in the capacity of note taker.

You will be given an opportunity to answer this allegation in full at the hearing and to put forward any mitigating circumstances that you feel should be taken into account. You are welcome to bring any supporting evidence which you feel may be relevant. You may also bring any witnesses to support your case.

You have the right to be accompanied in the meeting by a work colleague or trade union representative trained in the role of companion.

Please confirm that you are able to attend and whether you will be calling any witnesses. Please also let me know whether you wish to be accompanied by a colleague or trade union representative, so that the necessary arrangements can be made.

The outcome of this meeting may result in sanctions under the Company's disciplinary procedure, up to and including termination of your employment.

If you are dissatisfied with any sanction that is imposed as a result of this meeting, you will have the right to appeal.

Please do not hesitate to contact me if you have any queries about the contents of this letter.

Yours sincerely

[Name]
[Job title]

9. OUTCOME OF DISCIPLINARY MEETING LETTER

[Date]
[Employee name],
[Address]

Dear [Name]

I write to confirm the outcome of the disciplinary meeting held with you on [date]. The meeting was led by [name] and was also attended by [names of other attendees and their capacities].

[EITHER]
After carefully considering both the investigation evidence and your comments during the disciplinary meeting, it has been decided that:

You will be issued with a [state the sanction]. This warning will remain on your records for [number] months from the date of the disciplinary meeting.

As stated in the meeting, any further misconduct may result in further disciplinary action being taken and further sanctions being imposed, up to and including your dismissal from the company.

You are required to make the following improvements and your performance/conduct will be monitored over the coming months to ensure you meet these requirements:
[list requirements]

[INCLUDE, IF TRAINING IS REQUIRED:] [Name] will arrange the necessary training as requested by you in the meeting.

[OR]
After carefully considering both the investigation evidence and your comments during the disciplinary meeting, it has been decided that:

No disciplinary sanction will be imposed.

[IF APPROPRIATE] However, due to the concerns discussed with you, you are required to improve your conduct and it is expected that you will [outline expectations].

Your conduct will be monitored and reviewed on an ongoing basis.

Please be advised that if there are any further incidents of misconduct, you may be subject to formal disciplinary action.

[ALL]
If you are not satisfied with this decision then you have the right to appeal. Please write to [name] within [number of days per company disciplinary policy] days of receiving this letter explaining why you are unhappy with this decision. A meeting will then be convened to hear your appeal. As with the disciplinary meeting, you have the right to be accompanied at any appeal meeting by a work colleague or a trade union official trained in the role of companion.

Yours sincerely

[Name]
[Job title]

10. INVITATION TO APPEAL MEETING LETTER

[Date]
[Employee name]
[Address]

Dear [Name]

I am in receipt of your letter dated [insert date] in which you confirmed your wish to appeal against the outcome reached in respect of your [disciplinary/grievance] matter dated [date of decision].

Your appeal meeting will take place on [date] at [time] in [location]. The meeting will be conducted by [name], and [name] will also be in attendance to act as a note taker.

You have the right to be accompanied to the appeal meeting by a work colleague or trade union official trained in the role of companion. If you wish to do so, please let me know the name of your companion in order that we may be assured that they are aware of the nature of their role.

Please note that the decision at the appeal meeting will be final and there is no further right of appeal.

I would be grateful if you could confirm receipt of this letter and your attendance to the meeting.

Yours sincerely

[Name]
[Job title]

11. OUTCOME OF APPEAL MEETING LETTER

[Date]
[Employee name]
[Address]

Dear [Employee name]

This is to confirm the outcome of the appeal meeting held on [date] with regard to [outline details of warning imposed] issued to you on the [date].

At the meeting [you declined your right to be accompanied OR you were accompanied by [name]].

The reasons for your appeal were [insert reasons]. You also stated [detail mitigating factors offered].

I have given careful consideration to your submissions and have decided to [uphold the original decision OR reverse the decision OR change the decision]. My reasons for this are [insert reasons].

I would advise you that this decision is final and there is no further right of appeal.

Yours sincerely

[Name]
[Job title]

12. INVITATION TO GRIEVANCE MEETING

[Date]
[Employee Name]
[Address]

Dear [Name]

Further to your written grievance dated [date] of which I acknowledge receipt, I write to invite you to a meeting to discuss the matter. The meeting will be held on [date] at [location]. Hearing the meeting will be [name], and [name] will also be attending in the capacity of note taker. You have the right to be accompanied to the meeting by a work colleague or trade union representative trained in the role of companion. Please let me know as soon as possible the name of any companion you wish to bring to the meeting so that we can be assured of their understanding of the role.

The outcome of this meeting will be confirmed to you in writing.

If you are not satisfied with any decision awarded as an outcome of the meeting then you have the right to appeal. You have the right to be accompanied to an appeal meeting by a work colleague or trade union official trained in the role of companion. Please contact me if you wish to discuss any of the above or if you have any queries relating to the grievance procedure.

Yours sincerely

[Name]
[Job title]

13. OUTCOME OF GRIEVANCE MEETING

[Date]
[Employee name]
[Address]

Dear [Name]

I write to confirm the outcome of the grievance meeting held with you on [date] by [name]. We have carefully considered the grievance you have raised and
[EITHER]
have decided to turn down your grievance for the following reasons [state reasons].
[OR]
have decided to uphold your grievance and suggest the following course of action to resolve the issue: [give details of the suggested course of action/persons responsible/timescales/conditions].
[ALL]
If you are unhappy with this decision you have the right to appeal. If you wish to do so, please refer your grievance in writing to [insert name, job title] within [insert number of days] working days of the date of this letter. Arrangements for a further hearing will then be made.
You have the right to be accompanied to the appeal meeting by a colleague or trade union representative trained in the role of companion. Following the appeal, the decision will be communicated to you in writing and this decision will be final.

If you have any queries about this decision, please do not hesitate to contact me.

Yours sincerely

[Name]
[Job title]

INDEX